Copyright © 2023 by the Author
Published By: Sandpiper Records
ISBN: 978-1-916838-13-0
Printed in the United Kingdom by
Biddles Books Limited
First Printing Edition, 2023

TRAMPLED UNDERFOOT

Antony S Thomas

Foreword

Over three decades ago, I walked into the West Glamorgan Health Authority School of Nursing to begin a new chapter of my life. In 1990, you could start nurse training at 18, and at 26 years old, I was significantly older than the fresh-faced group of eager young trainees assembled around the rickety and dusty classroom that was to be our academic base for the best part of three years.

A shark can detect 1 part of blood in 1 billion parts of water. If, for reasons best known to yourself, you prick your finger in the sea, good old Jaws will lock on to that single drop of claret at less than a mile away, and you better hope the toothy fucker has just eaten, or you have a canister of compressed air and a rifle handy if he hasn't.

I've always been blessed, or possibly cursed, with a similarly finely tuned mirth radar. If even the mere potential for a laugh to be had is present, it sets my senses on edge, and I'm drawn to the source like a moth to a flame. The instinct has to be acted upon immediately. I don't even know it's happening, but it will, and there's no point trying to resist it, even if it's at significant personal or professional cost.

You'd have more joy telling your kidneys to *"take the weekend off."* So, I must let nature take its course and enjoy the ride.

Seated at the opposite end of the room was another student about the same age as me. I had never met him before and knew nothing about him. I don't remember how Antony "Tom" Thomas, a working-class, left-leaning, principled, and thoughtful firebrand, ended up sitting next to Kevin Jones, a North Walian, politically homeless, impulsive, and car crash personality, for the duration of our training, but I do remember that it all happened within about a nanosecond. and my life has been markedly richer as a result.

So, if I were to write my memoirs of nurse training, I would remember absolutely nothing that I was taught over those three years, but I do remember literally crying with laughter on a daily basis.

What's the best thing for a head injury?

Is it a baseball bat?

It is genuinely one of the few times in my life when it was a pleasure to go to work, and that's because of who had exclusive access to my ear.

Nothing and no one was safe from our search for fun.

A bad-tempered surgeon was reduced to tears after Tom hid one of his theatre clogs in a linen basket (not both; that wouldn't have been a thousandth as funny), never to be seen again. A battle-axe ward sister had her photograph, proudly displayed at a hospital entrance, replaced with a cartoon of everyone's favourite liver chomper, Hannibal Lector, in his full serial killer regalia.

We would terrorise lecturers and classmates alike, normally responding to faux earnestness or pomposity, but often because, well, it's a laugh, isn't it?

We created a mountain of hand-drawn cartoons because that was the fastest medium to share a joke without speaking out loud.

On one occasion, a drawing was literally eaten to avoid it falling into *enemy hands*. This incident remains up there in the top ten funniest things I've ever experienced.

Fast forward 33 years, and the comedic gravity that bound us together remains. I look back at pivotal moments and can't help but laugh out loud.

From the time we worked together at the medical centre at Port Talbot Steelworks. *The facility that time forgot* was situated so far below the radar that virtually nobody even knew it was there.

This meant 8-hour shifts, where the normal stimulation of patients, or indeed, human contact, was removed, meaning we found more outlandish and outrageous ways to amuse ourselves, which we achieved with flying colours ….I do hope there's a chapter about what we did with the kettle.

To quote Tom, the only thing that could improve this job *was if a bikini-clad supermodel paid us in crisp notes as we left the building.*

We spent many years holding season tickets at Vetch Field, supporting Swansea City. Once again, I cannot recall a single goal, save, passage of play, or league position, but I can remember every 90 minutes being filled with laughter so joyous that the regret I feel that I will never experience these days again borders on the physical. The very best of times.

A friend of mine once met astronaut Neil Armstrong. Eager to engage such a bona fide legend in conversation, but not to go down the tiresome *Hello mate. What's it like on the moon, then?* route, he chose the following question as his opening gambit:

"Mr. Armstrong, who inspires you?"

Armstrong thought for a few seconds before replying.

"Ordinary people, or normal people, live the most interesting and extraordinary lives."

That answer has stuck with me ever since. I've met a lot of normal people in my life, and even the gentlest of surface scratches universally reveal that they have a fabulous story to tell, which is easily interesting enough to justify putting pen to paper. Tom is more than an ordinary person, so I know you'll enjoy this book.

He's had an interesting life, and I'm not sure I've ever heard Tom say something that wasn't worth hearing. It'll make you think. It'll transport you to familiar places along with those you don't recognise; but listen, you'll enjoy the ride, and don't we all like a mystery tour now and again?

But most of all , he knows how a joke works so you're going to have one hell of a laugh.

Kevin Caswell-Jones
North Wales - Aug 2023
Z-list stand-up comedian
Him out of Viz.

Prologue

Here we are then. Sedentary in the pleasing arboretum of a cancer therapy ward, hooked up to a trickling cascade of venomous chemicals and saline irrigation. Over-jollified nurses and a locus of determined heart that crushes any Californian faith healer sanctorum with their stupid gong baths and chakra-balancing fanny incense. Let's exploit your sympathy gland.

The mind re-routes from why I'm here, and what's happened to my presumed immortality. A small vein at the dorsal of my right-hand pulses an ephemeral cadence as the drip-drip-drip of toxicity commissions a suicide mission to seek out and diminish the dark neoplasms that lie in wait at the hazardous *Liver Sector*. Thoughts scatter away from what sits as mundane to convulsing brilliant shapes of things. Oblique event traffic from passing times. *'The Numskulls'* in Beezer comic would simply have despatched a jovial worker with a lump hammer and shovel to deal with all this cancer nonsense.

You hold in your hand (not that hand, the other one, saucy) a compendium of arbitrary. A bio-haphazard leap across epochs of reverie. I could fake highbrow and cloud you in the pretence. But the reality of the moments are no different from any night out with your old schoolmates, when the laughs, controversy, jeopardy and apocryphal mayhem come flooding back - mostly in Dolby remasters that over-embellish the original clatter, and put in extra hiss. These are the best moments. The cherished moments. The dirty moments. We all taste the same essences, albeit cooked up in a different broth. That must be what it's like when all your memories flash by like a sped-up movie of motorway tail-lights at night.

What is it that reclines us in elysian fields cloaked in the dew of dog piss, styrofoam and e-coli? We shadow box with abstracts, while the silhouettes test our instincts: fear, hunger, revulsion, insomnia, joy, love, introspection, hallucination, enlightenment. The list is as endless as the drones of insects at dusk. Sometimes we need herbal and chemical taxis to get us there, but the terminus is uncertain and exciting in equal measure.

As is the expectation in recounting tales of yore, surfing amidst the spindrifts of an ever-changing orient; some of the language in this book will undoubtedly fail the cultural *scratch 'n' sniff test of time*. And a good thing too. Perhaps tales of destruction in an 80s Chinese restaurant, or the horrific late-70s spectacle of *the Big Bladder* deserve to be stashed in a hidden subterranean depository like some antiquated Saxon horde. But one day, someone will unearth it, so we may as well hold it to our bosoms now, despite the language of the epochs from whence they were created. Even *"On the Buses"* can still be found somewhere on satellite TV. Anyway, it all disperses into yellowing pages over time or melts into the desecrated pixels of an e-reader that's spent its throwaway lifespan slipping continually from oily hands over a hotel balcony. So, if I do get cancelled for dinosaur thoughts chiselled on the walls of time caves, disclaimer: it's your fault for buying it in the first place.

Let us draw days of amalgam where events collide, spiralling in a hall of mirrors. The reflections are sometimes perceptible. Memory cabinets are tipped onto the floor, and I scramble to put the clutter back in place.

My stories are mostly *of* and from *then,* sprinkled with contemporary embellishment.

Baron Munchausen would maybe call it *magic dust.* You may pick up the faecal notes of a cynical old trot existing under the spirit guidance of a blemished cherubim. And who could blame you? Even if you do get a few laughs on this journey (why are even the most benign things that we take for granted called *a journey* these days? I'm having another piece of toast or nipping upstairs for a pee. Neither are journeys. But you can bet that a Sunday supplement *lifestyle and culture* influencer named Aubergine will beg to differ). And it is a journey. A varying travelogue of cognisance. Those who were part of these fables will identify changed names and probably dispute these outlandish fables, fuelled by the South Wales tradition of *gorliwio* (exaggeration). Creative licence, boyos.

Wait! There's a bleeping sound. My drip needs changing. Carry on without me. I'll catch up.......

Chapter 1: The Shorthand of Emotion

Robert Browning once wrote, *"Who hears music, feels his solitude peopled at once."* I'm sure that's what we all had in mind when we made our eye-widened travels to halls and fields and pubs and farms and beaches and clubs in randomised recurring unison like the atonal zombies that we are. Otherwise, why would we spend every scratched penny nestling amidst the fluff and Polo fruits of our denims to watch a gig somewhere? Anywhere. The importance of music as a balm for our hollow souls can range from sticking your head in a Sabbath PA bin, the beautiful pulsing grace of Steve Reich, the fractious melancholic sonar of Sandy Denny, or your Nan quietly thrusting a 50p record token in your hand as if the two of you were conducting a low-level smack deal in the lanes behind her house. *And don't tell your Grampa.* Soothsayers abound. Some on county lines.

An old friend and I were reminiscing about those halcyon days in the 70's when we all felt emboldened in our purposely-ripped punk cottons to sneer at a park keeper to fuck off, but reacted in polite clipped tones whenever we were at a mate's house to listen to albums or leaf through a Hipgnosis catalogue of vinyl art, and his mam came in offering tea and biscuits around the din of Beefheart.

But this isn't just some madeleine cloud of whimsy echoing an ergophobic life of couch-surfing enveloped in landfills of music and movies. We did sometimes *go outside*. 1977 was, after all, another baking summer; and led to myriad weekend treks to the coast to swim, drink, smoke, and generally arse about in a pond amidst the sand dunes like we were Californian sophomores on a T-Bird holiday wankathon. In reality, we were council estate lads paddling in our pants with newts and discarded Strongbow cans snagged amidst the *Lurgy Pool* weeds, before drying off in an old workman's hut with a makeshift wood burner and several crusty-thumbed copies of Fiesta.

Magical times made even more wondrous as my Grundig MW radio coughed itself alive into the static rebound of Alan Freeman's *Saturday Rock Show*. None of us ever really believed that old 'Fluff' was a rock fan; but amidst all the operatic jingles and catchphrase bombast, the show provided some daytime relief to the astonishing corn of maladroit music-haters like DLT, or the impenetrable transatlantic guff of Emperor Rosko. In those brief capsules of time, we experienced freedom, music, hope, and sunstroke. Fluff gave us Rory Gallagher in a world where the name *'Thatcher'* was satisfyingly meaningless.

Let's talk of *freedom*. A word that has been polluted by inflated interests over time. The planet has opened, only to shrink its distance in turn. Let's go back 4 years more. A junior school kid with the bedsheets over his head, tuning into a tiny shortwave radio in the bleak late hours after John Peel's show had faded away the last bars of *'Picking the Blues'* by Grinderswitch imbued with the ambience of frost crackling on the broken window seals and the clanking of Corona pop bottles at the foot of the bed filled with hot water. The radio picked up the shortwave white noise refrain of barely audible bleeps from a Soviet spy outpost or the feint chiming of Cretan balalaika cross-mixed in static with a live Flemish debating chamber. The sort of soundpool magpie food that sampling DJs will pay a King's ransom for these days.

But why is it important? As another good friend of mine once mused, "*If a band or football team wants to play somewhere, that's their fucking business, not ours. We should keep our noses out.*" And wallet, evidently. Relationships and gate-crashing a party are analogous to our engagement with the arts. The deduction is that we put all our fragile emotional states into the hands of those we adore, gaining a feint waft of nirvana from their pheromone embrace, only to be smashed repeatedly on the rocks of disillusionment at a turnpike where we mistakenly thought they really loved us. Everyone leaves us one day. But our favourite bands never fully desert us; they just become horrible, fire-damaged mannequin xeroxes of what first brought us together. For all our loyal frailties, why do we not reflect on the many ways in which they betray us? Perhaps *we should keep our noses out.* But why do we keep coming back, covering up the bruises so nobody can perceive the abuse we've endured? When do we clear the obsessive tear-caked mascara sleep dirt from our eyes and lumpen, hurt wax from our ears?

Is it when a band fragments into a vapour of bulimic intoxication; leaving a nodule-throated frontman to head for the open kindergartens of idée-fixed nubiles, becoming pastilled-up like a German hospital DJ with a bleached anus who runs aqua aerobics on a weekend team-building conference in Alicante? Meanwhile, bygone tales of groupie plastercasts become artisan mirth trees grown from the mandrake roots of urban legend. So they wander off to the worm bosom of poltroonery, spewing demented reactionary conspiracies on an alt-right media outlet for man-babies. But one day they return to regenerate their pension schemes, looking and sounding like hideous panegyric approximations made from tallow. And they know that we'll devour it in the gaping jaws of our wallets.

Is it during a anaphylactic reaction to palming our doting outreached candle-clutching hands, triggering an ectoplasmic bukkake, whereby the former satanic moon cadaver mesomorphs into a moron-channelling piñata of every tweed fret-buzzing hotel band with an endless catalogue of AOR-friendly soporifics? I felt the rain down in Africa. *I told you to book a fucking villa in Tuscany, didn't I? Stupid twat.* They have anaesthetised us to innovation. Fed us a microwaved digest of inertia.

A beam of light sucks up our lost heroes, probes their mucky cavities, clones them, and drops the hollow replicants back through the Earth's atmosphere, armed with a strumming morass of balladeering vomitus for a new generation of star-crossed idiots to fork out hundreds to put on their anniversary playlist or plastic weep death anthem. Alive and a damn good kicking.

Most sepia-ravaged rock zealots with an LP collection hewn with the dust, beer stains (or seminal fluid, if you owned a copy of Roxy Music's *Country Life* album), and roach burns of passage will have their own tick-box of quail. We will pinpoint the intimate feelings of treachery when we looked to those gods to soundtrack our whimsical sagas from adolescence into adulthood, and suddenly found they were every bit as fallible in life as we were. It's a delusional royalist bedecked in Empire tea towels, discovering that His Majesty has sweetcorn in his shit like the rest of us. Let's go with the flow.

Pandering to the tonal emptiness of every 6th form rugby fuckwit, every be-permed frowning debutante, and every disinterested moron who found culture to be a grating disruption to their ambitious, self-centred, joyless existences. To them, music is a novelty. A thing to control, monetise, or ban. A refuge for the *woke*. A badge to wear at a party that neither you nor I would frequent. If we were ever invited in the first place.

Fickle partisans can take their business elsewhere and excavate new avenues of gratification; serving notice that their icons' services are no longer required. Others get devoured by the deceit, hear mocking voices, and burst into stately piles plausibly owned by their heroes; armed to the teeth, with the smell of blood on their cracked lips and a spiralling head full of tunes rotating backwards at 16 RPM. But do our heroes give a toss? Maybe they didn't want to be hoist (or, in later life, winched) under hot stage lights threatening that flammable lacquered back-comb wig. Perhaps they just wished for normality away from the greasepaint, exploding TV sets and dogfish-based carnal mythology. I know it. I witnessed it first-hand.

I'm thinking of a hot summer's day, probably in 1990, when I took my bulgingly-pregnant wife for a spin down to the exhausted shoreline of Porthcawl. A place where Hell's Angels once held dominion in a dingy rock pub enclave; now the home to shuffling burnouts of paucity and the trembling veers of mobility scooters rattling in semi-collapse under the absurd weight of their riders. Some clad in *Sons of Anarchy* smocks. The converging circuit to a pie shop nods a slo-mo homage to *Ben Hur,* in polyester and badly-inflated tyres. Driving along the fagged-out seafront; I cast my eyes to the Pavilion to amuse myself at the hulling posters heralding an objectionable clam bake of yesterday's TV stars scratching their haunted souls for divinity. Plus, *Singles Night: Sunday 8PM.*

To digress, I once went there for the latter with friends in search of some *jest and obligation-free sex,* and encountered what can only be described as a Darwinian control group. The furrowed expression and gasps of wonderment the old beardy evolutionary exhaled when he first set down on the Galapagos must have mirrored our gamut of baffled visages as we found ourselves corralled in a cork-panelled function room with the cast of *Eraserhead.* Oversized kipper ties scaffolding forceps-induced heads that shrivelled like a child's forgotten beachball; wooden legs with real feet; squeaking voodoo doll-women approaching in a vapour of grinning malfeasance traduced by a pulsating hump or arm twitch. The flickering neon light at the bar serving only to illuminate and eradicate in equal measure the eyes and spittle from pointing warped figures in the shadows, orienting this carnival of souls towards the curiosity of fresh meat.

But anyway, back to the *Percydote* (or *a complete pack of bullshit*), as it's so rightly weaponised to throw at me in times when I forget that I'm only 5% as cool as I think I am. My wife and I were heading past the Pavilion of Screams when I spotted Led Zeppelin's Robert Plant sitting casually in the doorway, eating what looked to be an ice cream cone. Now, I yield to nobody in my long unrequited love for *The Zep* and how, despite my over-compensating heterosexuality, I would willingly offer myself up as a banquet for the whole band to devour at their fabled leisure, or in

Plant's case, as a NME journalist once described him: *a self-satisfied carnal gourmet.*

Ignoring the plight of my 7 months' distending spouse, I jammed my foot down hard on the brakes as if I'd spotted an infant chasing a balloon between parked vehicles, leaving a lengthy discordant squawk not unlike the theremin screams on *Whole Lotta Love.* Grey tyre smoke chemtrailed my abrupt halt on the roadside as I exited the car and marched purposefully over to address my great idol, 30 meters away.

I've since discovered an obscure scientific formula, which recognises that *adulatory obsession divided by distance travelled = temporary neural and physiological paralysis.* I was but 5 yards away and approaching, and my trachea was seizing up in direct proportion to the fear-dilation of my anus. A quick cough as I approached, and I felt a warm droplet of wee appear. Plant paused his cornet, flicked a thick lock of perfect Norse hair away from his brow, and looked up, presumably in expectation of a captivating or profound aphorism worthy of a Great Sage. I was frozen in what must have been presented to poor Bob as the maniacal rictus of a serial strangling homunculus who'd just been jettisoned from window licking the sunshine coach. Another empty hack of the chest to disrupt the drying tumbleweeds that were passing the moment. I reached inside me to rip out those wizened scrolls of philosophy lodged somewhere in a deep laryngeal cave. Fuck! I've got them! Yes! Speak! Now! DO IT!.... I coughed and pointed at him.

"Er, ahem...clirch.... w-w-w-what flavour is it?". A baffled Percy frowned fleetingly to ponder the great nugget that had just rolled upon him, peered momentarily at his melting repast, and fixed me with an azure-eyed gaze. *"Vanilla, of course."* With those three words came a thunderclap of dismay and bleakness. Three words smashing to the boundaries my inane thumbless off-spin. *Vanilla ...of course.* What flavour is it? *What flavour is it? What flavour is it? What flavour is it? Vanilla, of course.* The librettos orbited my world of dumb, painting an illusory carousel of lame unicorns jockeyed by the dead cast list from decades of Pavilion shows, gesticulating mockingly back at me.

We could have debated the many majesties of music and folklore and ended the day as great friends, leap-frogging like children on the pavilion flagstones, vowing to be inseparable; leaving our wives and forever sitting side-by-side on twin granite thrones overlooking the Black Mountains; our opium heads bursting with the furtive colours and tongues and sacred chords of ancient shamen carrying us up to the enlightened rulership of advanced civilisations existing in parallel to our own worlds, unimaginable to all but those who glimpse their dancing worm shadows briefly in the salient pools at the corners of their eyes. Instead of slinking off to my car, broken on the rocks of dejection like a humiliated cock-fighter cradling the limp remains of his prize bantam. I slumped into my seat.

"What happened?" quizzed my wife, espying my ashen manifestation. *"Don't ask."* was the barely-audible squeak of tears as I clunked at the gearstick and pulled away in a cortege half gear of quelling grief. *"He's Smiling. Looks like he's enjoying that ice cream"* she said, fatally twisting the knife into my already gaping wound of shame.

The Man from Neath

Skinny Jeans, runny nose
Love grows, see my Rolex it glows.
Instagram-influencer-ready
Now it's last orders he staggers, unsteady.
Hair of the dog at 8:30
Down for a grope at Neath Workies
She swears she's only thirty
But her breath smells of beef jerky, stuck under her teeth
Any port in a storm for the Man from Neath.

Skinny jeans, sunbed verruca
A vertigo tower of flaming sambucas.
Tombstoning in a used mankini
Drives his car like he's in the Sweeney.
Sunday dinner in Briton Ferry
Cops a roundhouse kick from a tramp named Terry
But he don't care if it's lamb or beef
It's gentleman's relish for the Man from Neath.

Skinny Jeans half-sleeve tattoo
Found these flowers off a lamppost for you.
Ran from a foodbank with some tiger bread
Stole three slabs from Fred West's shed.
Got seasick on Nan's waterbed
(Some things are better left unsaid)
…And definitely unseen
With the doggers spot at Jersey Marine.
But what's that cold hand underneath?

He's touchy feely is The Man from Neath.

Skinny Jeans, hairy back
I shat in your hot-tub, just for the craic
You won't have me down for a party pooper
I lost my cherry to a starship trooper.
But when all things are said and done
I'll send you a text asking, "you OK, hun?"
We'll sail Tonna canal for those extra thrills
Back to my man-cave for a Netflix and chill.
Because I'm a man of means, neither famine nor feast.
Step inside, love. I'm the Man from Neath.

Chapter 2: Over the Hills and Far Away

It wasn't the first time that a signpost to all things Zep would plunge me into cognitive upheaval, leaving neural scars like the barnacle skin of a well-travelled porpoise. Knebworth Festival, August 4th, 1979, embedded a lasting memory baked of wonder, bewilderment, and outright cataclysm. UK festivals are common articulations as bedfellows with urine-basted triple-cooked mud and long trenches of slow gravitational shit rivulets edging their relentless way slowly to some hellion sump. And even the journey itself can sometimes be fraught with ungodly threat. Our annual voyages to Glastonbury and Reading in the late 70s/early 80s embraced a list that to young punters of today, would seem like describing a Brueghel or Hogarth triptych to a squeamish school of the blind, whose only touchstone would be the spoors of decay. Survival role-playing has never felt or tasted so good. Or bad, if the accumulated layers of moss on your teeth could be analysed.

But if this was normalising the experience, then the tribe I hooked up with for Knebworth were of the Berserker breed. The most hirsute perspiring frottage of oily double-denim brigands that would ever secrete from south Wales like madcap Silurian hazard beacons. Crammed into the aluminium windowless meat shed of a rented box van weighed down by crates of booze, smoking apparatus, and pernicious weaponry, we were shuttered in by Larry the driver, who exhorted: *"Right, you twats. Once we'se on the M4, there's no stoppin' until Knebworth. So fuck off!"* Trapped inside our unlit, rattling metal oubliette, we scrambled like Papillon roaches to find the most comfortable place propped up by our sleeping bags wrapped around 24 cans of Skol per head that were already diminishing at a frenetic rate, along with a daunting all-you-can-eat buffet of psilocybin and chunks of Red Leb laid out like a bacchanal platter on a big tray of Baco-foil. We'd only voyaged about 20 miles.

As the moon turns the tides, so does the kidney's osmotic passage from beer to urine. Knowing that Larry wasn't going to be stopping; ingenuity and innovation were vital. Luckily, we had some of the finest minds known to bikerdom -and presumably, prison survivalism. Now, I'm not embellishing this saga with scenes of catheterisation or rudimentary dialysis from reconditioned exhaust piping; but am merely illustrating how we overcame being billeted in a large alloy cube without pissing in each other's mouths. Thus, the professorial amongst us ruminated and came up with a virtuoso solution: *'The Big Bladder'*, a large 5-ply binbag (as opposed to those gossamer-thin garbage holders of today, which wouldn't hold more than a crisp packet before rupturing like a hornet brood angrily exiting its egg chamber). This was tethered to the van's internal framework, into which one would urinate, and the carry handles immediately reaffixed to its moorings.

'*Genius*' I hear you exhort. Yes, if you were over 5ft 8in tall, and male.

The perilous navigation of indignity in the quest for a pee by the two diminutive girls in our troupe was enough to disinfect any belief systems of gender reassignment. Thus, Sue had to squat precariously over an elevated fissure, while Karen held her balance, standing on a small tower of cans. The rest of us averted our gaze as if subjected to a Balkan snuff movie, or when a cashier theatrically looks away while you enter your PIN (but still compelled to have a sneaky peak through one eye for a penurious glimpse of fanny). '*The Big Bladder*' was living famously up to its illustrious moniker.

Turning off the M4 onto the A-roads and into the Berkshire countryside was something we hadn't quite factored in, as a final act to Larry's Hanoi helicopter driving. The unheralded flip to a dual carriageway winding its way to Chalfont and beyond will live with me forever as a journey of pure, unbridled horror.

We were expecting some bumps and twists in the road; but not the way Larry was throwing us about. We resembled the cheap visual trick used in the 60's TV sci-fi series, '*Voyage to The Bottom of The Sea*', where the camera would tilt on its side and the cast would run from starboard to port to make it look like the submarine had just been headbutted by a towering radioactive whale-man with arms like the trunks of sequoia, or some extra-terrestrial plasma discharge from an enraged plankton race. Verily, we rolled to and fro like an empty cider can reorienting the seaside winds. We imagined Larry; lit roly in mouth, cackling like a cheap movie villain. But there's always one who never obeys the rules of physics. Always one who walks into a burning building just as everyone else is leaving and beating out the flames in their hair. Always one who insists that the B-sides of every hit single were so much better, but was too fucking wasted to recall which ones. In this case, it was Dafydd, a brown-toothed sweary contrarian, who stood there, arms crossed, in a gape of defiance from central casting as a podgy sawn-off Wrangler-clad inebriate. *"Stop being twats!"* he exalted, just as Larry thrust a slalom through deviating cones, violently propelling Dafydd into *The Big Bladder.*

That moment of frozen acuity, which sedates eye movement and flips the world on a gyre. That Matrix sense of standing still while everything else erupts around you at kung fu hyper-speed. Eruption indeed. A cascading magma of warm putrefying piss prolapsed through a foot-sized blinking aperture in the plastic black viscera and out amongst the terrified throng as a cosmic arterial geyser. Giant rivulets of renal-processed lager pumped relentlessly upon us. We couldn't run from it, and the more agile could only lift themselves above the wretchedness on box struts, before lactic acid speared their weakened boozy frames, and they plunged back into a shin-deep riptide from the Islets of Langerhans.

Disbelief transmuted to panic. That Waco sense of enclosure as the bullets zing by, and the building burns. A pause to reset before the fight or flight mechanism kicks in. Swilling about like traumatised sādhus and sādhvīnes on a Ganges funeral riffle, we thumped, kicked, scratched and head-butted the aluminium frontier between us and our resolute chauffeur; imploring Larry to stop the bloody van.

"I told you twats a million times. I ain't stopping until we gets to Knebworth. Now pipes the fuck down!"

"But there's piss everywhere. We're dying!"

"I don't gives two fucks, mun. We's not stopping. Them's the fucking rules."

In an evolving sense of fatalist guild, we managed to prise the rear shutter up to a sufficient breach, allowing the foaming eddy of micturition to gush from the van onto the road like the berating mouth of a dying robot. Relief for our urea-rinsed ankles; not so much for any cyclist in our slipstream.

Knebworth. The stately retreat for expanding waistbands wishing punk rock away like it was a wasp in a phone booth. A hairy white male extravaganza of sloth, hubris and fluff (that's the title of the next book sorted). This swollen pustule was best exemplified in the form of Ronnie Woods' New Barbarians. A promotional circle jerk. A scabrous, dilated, drunken damp fag pastiche of pals that staggered on 2 hours late, and ground through a relentless discord of stupefying dross that wouldn't pass muster as a comedy tribute act. By far the worst band I have ever seen in my life, indoors and outdoors. And I've seen Uriah Heep.

Best not to even attempt chronicling the festival much further (even if that was the lowest bar). A difficult reportage when the August sun starched our bladder-cracked paws, as denims putrefied and a trillion heatwave greenflies swarmed to greet a siren call to their nasal sonar. For *Zeppanistas* alike, it was a stunning event, not a musical one. Messrs. Page, Plant, Jones, and Bonham could have appeared as The Black and White Minstrels, continually stopping to juggle a solitary tangerine or swat a Chaffinch. It didn't matter. As living reflections of a dream, it was joyous light and sound to behold, akin to the very first time as an infant you entered a fairground. As a performance, it was a deconstructed mess of ambiguities and melancholy akin to the last ring hurrah of Muhammed Ali. Creaking with rust. Flabby, fearful, and ill-prepared, yet still radiating twinkles of enchantment to help us recall how momentous it all was to our young devoted lives. Even if we reeked of each other's piss.

Chas & Dave and Todd Rundgren (though not dropped together in an emergency bill-saving Cockney/

Philadelphian experiment) were excellent, by the way.
Runt, Rabbit, Runt, Rabbit, etc.

Chapter 3: I'm Not Worthy

The late-70's/early 80's festival scene was a different place from where it sits now. As with our towns, cities, and sporting venues; gentrification has siphoned the energy and turned it into a thematic pilgrimage where those with a keen sense of sharp elbows and magnetic eyes hot-wiring the clasp of daddy's wallet can now groove to some kitsch post-ironic piece of vaudeville on somebody's shoulders, baring their symmetrical American glares and faultlessly toned bodies to whichever TV camera is directed their sorry way. The whole shebang is now a bejewelled circle jerk; akin to those hideous Christian gatherings in Hyde Park, which we'd rather suture our throats to our arseholes than attend.

Be it *The Big Bladder*, a full demijohn of piss on an accurate trajectory towards the on-stage poseur, or a happy-clappy double peace-signalling girl in a MC5 t-shirt on the creaking shoulder of her boyfriend getting a beer can bouncing off her hyper-enthusiastic skull. It could be the relentless, slow gravitational march of feculence advancing down a field ditch on a tilted axis and into a sump of wretchedness, or a member of your gang snapping off a handy twig and plucking a tomato skin from his anus, before chasing you across a crowded festival sward. You won't read this on Ticketmaster's web portal.

Before it became the glowing beacon for white middle class displacement and selfie spangly-influencing on a bed of celeb felching, Glastonbury was the *Big One*. The trip we desired. Whereas our forebears had works-sponsored outings to Rhyl (and came home to find all the food and pets gone, and a gaping orifice where an overfilled bath had plummeted through the ceiling); we possessed the annual delirium of an early summer gathering in some west country meadows, evicting dairy cows in our revelry. Glasto's USP helix spun in an alternative reality to Knebworth, and particularly Reading, with its heavy twin carborators of party seven pissclouds and vaudevillian crotch rock. Reading was a thick, toasted crust orbiting a cow turd. Solid and alluring on the surface, but scratch through the strata and you'd uncover a gaseous core of maggots and crazed monocellular forms fighting for space, chewing, writhing, gulping, and expiring in its own mulch.

The astonishing accuracy of punters aiming tins of kidney water at the heads of the afore-mentioned shoulder jockeys should have been installed as an Olympic event. Continuing the equestrian theme, surely this must have more merit than a posh dancing horse? Knebworth wasn't really a festival at all, being a single-day jaunt where turgescent kyoothans like Floyd or Genesis could pad out their hedge funds on a colossal country pile in Hertfordshire.

Throw cans of piss at Glastonbury and you'd become the recipient of multiple wagging fingers and unison library tutting, which to a stoned entryist would evoke field recordings of a wallaby flock that just discovered Juicy Fruit. You'd be carted off to a stripy *gong bath* tent, where a robed grifter resembling Arthur Brown would orbit you with Tibetan vibrations as someone read incantations from a manuscript of alternative norms. Cynics would soon twig that these part-time shamen were really boat lacquer salesmen to *'Bullseye'* winners in their spare time, or dole bums hanging around Bargain Booze. The capricious would skip away from under their canvas isosceles, vowing never to lob a micturition-loaded aluminium grenade ever again.

Glasto has always dined out on its singularity. A beacon for cod, strangeness and charm (*another future book title - Ed),* nodding gratuitously to olde Albion while waving its naughty wand to stars obscured by light pollution and rainclouds. It mythologised the sun and planetary alignments just like any old peddler of Mesoamerican hokum. It created a homestead for gingivitic nomads eking out a living carving owl heads or screen-printing panels of zen for the bored rich wishing for illumination beyond the confines of their Hunter wellies. Lao Tzu once asked: *Do you have the patience to wait until your mud settles and the water is clear?* Evidently the dour old sod had a rare infusion of humour inspired by a downpour in Pilton during Van Morrison's awful pyramid stage set.

But nostalgia is fake. At best, it is a fabrication fermented by advertising gurus and politicians flogging us their olfactory stories about a nightjar haze of cycling maidens, warm beer, and cricket on the heath. At worst, it's a subliminal purification of all our inert prejudices, fears, and desires to reshape the world exactly *as we want*. While it's a safe place to retreat to when the panel is ablaze with anger, greed, corruption, pollution, and tyranny; it's also weaponised to promise a world that no longer exists; be it the cinnamon-sprayed kitsch of a New York Yuletide or the Nazi flummery of alpine fields tended by golden-tressed Übermensch. I'd like four buses an hour, numerous hospitals in my town, free swimming lessons for kids, well-tended municipal parks and sporting facilities, beer at 50p a pint, and the closure of charity shops and food banks due to a lack of need. I'm not holding my breath for an uplift to Nirvana, and neither am I going to storm the Senedd. I'm certainly not selling you inspirational vignettes printed within the fatty twine of a vaginal dreamcatcher. Unless you ask me to.

One always envisaged sun-drenched festivals of sublime music and arts, staffed and attended through delightful multiculturalism, not an ugly rain-soaked grotbag army of scabrous, faintly animated piles of oversized rags encasing skeletons with a veneer of green-hued dermis, free-passed as the rightful festival-goers of eld. And hippies are the worst of them. Absolute grifting bastards.

But isn't that the road the wayfarer of fantasy takes us down? Our rem states process and lock away memories every night. Even if it's a load of old bullshit fabricated and repainted over time, nostalgia is a scampish dog trailing bog roll that runs freely through our desultory thought offices; tipping over random memory tables and snuffling through the odd file of events to unearth the light of treasured days. Galleries unveil snapshots of us that fade in time. Glastonbury Fayre. An event defined by its own bloated mythology.

Even if Glasto appropriated from America the Aquarian age of azure-eyed mountaintop flower children holding aloft their '*carbonated drink with plant extracts*' and gleaming a joyous rictus of moisturised skin and alabaster teeth while fluffing us with desires to '*teach the world to sing*'; the hardened of us really knew that we were entombed in rainy England and the campers were slipping on their arses, grazing on mushrooms, trying to out-stare a sheepdog, and being discordant nuisances tooling circadian flatulence resonating from the one tooth in their torpefied heads that hadn't succumbed to the pleonexia of heroin addiction.

What Glastonbury did do—and still does well—was tap into the weirdness and esoterica of British culture that resided in the mind annexes of folk horror, cosmology, fever dreams, psychogeology, Celtic paganism, and Saxon mythology. It rolled along the promenades of archetypal 70s Britishness, stepping across stones of hippiedom, counter-culture, and anti-imperialism to saucy postcard nudity and unobtrusive shitting and shagging in the woods. And amidst all that was a superb cocktail of diverse, and at times stirring, underground music and fabulous headline acts that you'd rarely see anywhere else.

Each year, we had a ritualised preparation for the *CND Glastonbury Festival*. As per Knebworth (see previous chapter), it consisted of the obligatory essentials: sleeping bag. Family pack of sausage rolls. Enough cans from the cash & carry to scuttle a freighter. Stopping off at the local dealer's house for a pic'n'mix or herbal and chemical enhancements, in the days when dope came in fragrant chunks that resembled the charred remains of a tyre factory *insurance job*. My personal favourite was '*Red Leb*' - a milder gateway into the jeopardy palace of '*Moroccan Black*', and some tabs of acid, which for the most part were the duds of their own hubris, every bit as predictably shit as 15p Astra bangers or Uriah Heep (yes, them again). More Glastonbury later.

Chapter 4: Practically Assured Stability

Like music, drugs framed the transition from doe-eyed adolescence into hard-nosed teenage realism, sometimes stopping en-route to disembark for the connection to other, stranger worlds. It was a mere five-year journey from believing schoolyard myths that even looking at Anadin would lead to a lifetime of ruinous dependence, prison, and death. Or taking a puff from a kid's rotohaler meant that you'd be *addicted to asthma*. A short stop away from being convinced that mixing paracetamol with Pepsi would send you on a non-returnable oblivion trip. But like all skint working-class kids needing a kick from that cliched *humdrum* existence and dreaming of reaching herbal or chemical enlightenment (before today's world of nitrous oxide balloons), there would always be spurious options for gateway experimentation, starting with booze and fags, of course. We'd be sat on the banks of the Rhanallt stream, strewn bottles of Woodpecker at our feet, dragging on a menthol cigarette; the burning 4" stick gripped tightly between index finger and thumb across the palm, and a big superficial draw accompanied by a pained expression. This grimace was meant to make us look council estate hard, like John Thaw in The Sweeney, but was more akin to a bus driver with a scrotal rash.

Predictably, we'd follow the local myths of smoking baked banana skins, cinnamon sticks, or lengths of Trill. I recall going into a local pet shop, ordering some hemp seeds, and the old proprietor suspiciously looking me up and down in my grubby denims and the hooky Pink Floyd t-shirt I bought from the back pages of *Sounds,* and retorting: "*I hope you're not going to be growing that Marriage Yewanna with these.*" This must have set the tone for all future drug barons, and I'm sure that Pablo Escobar's early riches were based on the morality clause of a farmer going: "*You're not going to be snorting any of that stuff, are you?*".

More often than not, I vomited a lung trying out these absurd concoctions. Rites of passage to prelude hopeless acts of match fitness for the real stuff. Those chunky aromatic blocks of Middle Eastern resin were staple fare, and relatively easy to come by if you had an older mate who could get the stuff. For a young lad used only to igniting his oesophagus on Findus Crispy Pancakes, inhaling the warm, sweet smoke of hashish was a pleasing encounter. While we'll all attest to how it enhanced music and gigs (I once proclaimed The Wurzels to be "*fine world musicians hidden behind bales of yokel bullshit*", during a bank holiday barn gathering, and then immediately tried to snuff this dreadful conniption by pretending that my comments were stoner irony, as a jury of peers roared with fatal mockery). An episodic out-of-body intoxication from mixing a lump of Moroccan with lager and black, soundtracked by old Gong hippy Daevid Allen's eerie '*N'Existe Pas*' album. An ordeal of verisimilitude to match the time I repeatedly leapt into the air (during a gig by pioneering Canterbury pop proggers, Caravan) to catch floating clouds rising from a joint, from which my waggish pal had secreted one of those prank *'snow tablets'.*

Weed could be relied upon to counteract years of shyness; ripping the gate that imprisoned my humour gland right off its hinges and playing havoc with my libido. Standing adjacent to Jools Holland in the Swansea Top Rank urinals and laughing uncontrollably and cruelly. Libido-wise, it happened on the same night, when, in a mad reverie of over-enthused grooving to the astonishing Dr Feelgood, my hand found itself inescapably trapped inside the tight shorts of a student teacher. Anyway, I can't be hauled off to the clink retrospectively like some old Oscar-winning producer. I wasn't even 16 when this happened, M'lud.

Hash enhanced my senses with unreal pathways to excellence. To these ears, I have composed prodigious bass lines and formed beautifully adroit minimal piano pieces, only to forget them completely the next day. I've written poetry that would jerk Walt Whitman to consider a career in scaffolding, but when read back in the morning it's a scrawling landfill of inanity about potatoes and a wasp. However, to add some culture balance to this tale; the shining path of herbal essences reached its alcazar via the green baize of my local sports and social club. After partaking in some of Marrakesh's finest resin in the club bogs, it was the turn of my mate and I to have our usual clumsy 50p knockabout on the snooker table, as the real *grown-ups* with their monogrammed cue coffins waited grudgingly for us to lose interest by the time the 40-minute light timer clicked off. But something happened. As we set ourselves up to shoot, the pockets looked about 2 feet wide. We couldn't miss. Reeling off a couple of half centuries and practically soiling ourselves with laughter after every impossibly long pot, we cleared up the table and turned around to spot the whole lounge watching and applauding a *"brilliant contest."* Except for the *experts,* who sat there chewing their top lips, looking like a carnival of gurners freebasing alum, and mewling to the club committee about cheating. Fuck knows what could have happened if we'd hit the mushrooms.

Bill Hicks' view of psilocybin was: *"I'm glad mushrooms are against the law, because I took them one time, and you know what happened to me? I laid in a field of green grass for four hours, going, "My God! I love everything." Yeah, now if that isn't a hazard to our country...."* I knew of a secret farm field, where, in the formative months of Autumn, I would harvest a hefty tranche of psychedelic fungi. This psylocibin yield was a gateway for mirth, stupefaction, and terror in disproportionate measures of imbalance. We weren't posh or daft enough for *enlightenment.* As usual, I was the litmus test for anything new and beyond convention. So as I laid out a platter of caps on a mate's coffee table, the rest of the group waited for me to bolt a handful down, sitting there observing to assure themselves that I wouldn't abruptly sprout doom wings and project a vomitus of burning crude oil as I exited the window like a startled Pteranodon. Minutes passed, and apart from raucous laughter at nothing specific, the general consensus was that I had collected a pile of inert fungi, so they waded in. Someone set fire to a newspaper being read by a mate, who continued to peruse the raging broadsheet, while the rest of us stared at the transmundane vision enfolding before our bloodshot eyes. Maybe that's the daily actuality for Telegraph readers. How else can we explain it?

Following the parlour arson, a thickening cloud of delusion started to draw across my fevered brow, and I insisted that I be given a lift home immediately. From a dynamic risk-hazard perspective, this was a terrible folly, as my errant taxi driver was none other than the compadre who watched the giant newsprint fuse ignite in his hands. No sooner were we on the road to my asylum when we swerved across the carriageway, steering a course directly down the centre of the highway. *"Got to keep the white lines in the centre of the car, or we will surely die,"* he repeated, with a look of ashen terror as if he were reliving a fatal car wreck over and over. I curled up in the passenger seat, my brain a mixture of trauma and graveyard hilarity, as we ploughed a perfect equatorial furrow down the A48 amidst a soundtrack of lengthy beeping and profanity, with vehicles swerving towards grass verges and pavements. How we survived this quest is an absurdity that only traffic scientists who take their crash test dummies home for tea could comprehend.

I stood at my front door in paralysis; index finger hovering around the doorbell button as if I'd been suborned to act out a terrible initiation bloodlust driven by omertà. Anyway, my Mam had been watching from the kitchen window and summoned me in quickly, checking outside that nobody in the street had witnessed the family shame of what appeared to be an acute psychiatric episode. I can vaguely recall staring for ten minutes at what looked like a ham roll the size of a bin lid and laughing riotously at some tediously forgettable 70s mid-afternoon TV sofa-com starring Irene Handl, while my Dad shouted to Mam: *"He's not bloody right in the head, he's not!"*. Not sure if he was referring to me or Wilfred Pickles. I was hence despatched to bed to spend the next twelve hours reliving every neurosis and fever dream I'd experienced as a child. The room changing from dwarf cupboard to immense warehouse, an alarm clock that whistled like Guy Mitchell, and a portmanteau of 70's Public Information Films, where instead of electrocution while rescuing a frisbee from an electrical sub-station, featured *The Spirit of Dark and Lonely Water* standing next to a tombstone with my name and date of death chiselled on it, replete with an echoing Patrick Allen voice-over warning: *"Never eat magic mushrooms in large quantities."* I guess Bill and I must have tried some very different fungi.

Chapter 5: All Gates Open

Mike, our Glastonbury driver, was less of a cold-blooded attack mercenary than Knebworth Larry, an elsewhither that suited us well. Even if the former was wasted before he even took the wheel and bumped the van as soon as we set off. Mike may have been leaving a soporific chemtrail, lurching across lanes and brushing hedgerows; but by fuck, his geniality shone like a beacon to illuminate our impending demise amidst the quotidian Somerset tractors and torpid sightseers dribbling along the meandering by-ways of the A37 and A361, in the days before dogging was invented.

But if preparation for Glasto was manifest, it was merely a staging post for the martial precision of entering the festival itself. Mike would park the van about 400 metres from the festival site, and we would pile out to emboss ourselves amidst the foliage at an unobtrusive corner of the fields. Worthy Farm in those days was surrounded by traditional agricultural hedgerows no higher than the average adult, meaning that it was easy to climb over, provided you were mindful of the layers of embedded blackthorn. It merely required us to drape a few sleeping bags over and crush a sizeable indent with our combined pile-on body weight, thus creating a bespoke entry point. It was then a simple act of walking across the meadows to the festival fields, following previous footpaths in the crops. Meanwhile, Mike and his girlfriend entered through the main area, parked up, and we then assembled like low-ranking cartel members to transfer our cargo onto the campsite. Twelve would travel for the price of two tickets and a few quid each for petrol; long before the construction of *Stalag Luft Pilton*, with its double-layered security borders patrolled by dog-handling steroidal heavies from Mossad, or whatever corporation commissions these steroidal joy-killing cage fighters these days.

I think what hit me the most about Glastonbury, as a 16-year-old from a council estate in the ash-belching aorta of industrial south Wales, was the scale, multiplicity, and prevailing oddness of it all. This bewildering dissimilitude of a citadel of otherworldly citizens was disconcerting as much as it was a stimulating bellwether of styles and cultures. Gawping at the hardcore flock of shamen, hippies, anarchist punks and motorheads, plus a large-hatted man wandering the big tents with a giant fake penis (*'The Glastonbury Prick'*), spraying all and sundry with brackish fluid. I felt that in all those primrose years I'd simply been going through the motions in ripped denims (which my Mam always fucked-up by putting patches on the inside of the deliberately torn apertures). Back-brushing my hair to look like a roady from the Pink Faeries, filing off the pointy bit of a safety pin to pretend it had pierced my lip, and going on the school outing to the Bath Old Vic in a *'Rock Against Racism'* tee. It was all bullshit cosplay. A prelapsarian whim. A join-the-dots agitation with one hand clutching Melody Maker, and the other wanking rapidly at the memory of the drunken English teacher sitting on my lap during *'The Merchant of Venice'*, and I caressed the lustrous veneer of her deluxe stockinged thigh.

There was no such grace and favour here on Worthy Farm. In 1943, Abraham Maslow, formulated *'The Hierarchy of Human Needs'*, which detailed a continuum upon which we all scrabble to reach a form of psychosocial Eden. This includes physiological, safety and cognitive needs. The latter need was perceptibly embraced by our unflagging gourmandism, imbibing, and intemperance. But let us concentrate on the former two rungs, as they apply exclusively to the *Glastonbury experience.*

Anyone who's experienced the vegetable curry at Glasto, washed down with a demijohn of local farm scrumpy (more about that later), will reveal sagas involving gastrointestinal calamity and lost hours staring at the stars in a stygian fugue of cramps and dehydration, questioning why your friend's teeth smell like a dead dog. A heady concoction of elephantine vats of lentil vindaloo poured into flimsy cups by a barmaid who could have been Poly Styrene's bigger harder sister, and plastic gallons of suede-hued fermentation of jonagold drowning in a quag of perdition that looked like a diabetic's catheter sack. This enteric tag team set off an express line from stomach to arsehole that sent you into a nosediving spiral of ferdutzt shitting psychosis.

You found yourself at an arse-clenching crossroads where a duodenal djinn juggled the cards of chance that would frame your weekend. Do you clench and hope it goes away? Surrender to the advance with incontinent abandon and lose your friends and dignity for life? Or do you dare to face the daunting Gehenna fortress -more commonly known as *'The Glastonbury Toilets'*? For the uninformed or uninitiated, before the spoilt days of tanker-sucked asepsis and sawdust sanitising, the Glasto bogs were a favela of conjoined shacks snaking along the contours of the fields; within each sat a plank with a football-sized aperture for you to evacuate your disturbances. There was no flush. The stinking extravasate would drop into a trench of unspeakable foulness, and follow a gravitational march, presumably towards some massive off-site abyss. Notwithstanding the smell and fume from thousands of evacuating colons, there must surely have been an explosive risk from the congregating methane and a casually-tossed joint. The ascending vapour probably punched a thermal hole in the Pilton stratosphere and caused extensive flooding along the Somerset levels. When a butterfly flaps its shitty wings, etc. But the true horror was reserved for anyone who dared to peek down into the mire out of curiosity (which we all do when completing a *number two,* like we're expecting to see an effigy of Che Guevara or Mother Theresa weeping amidst the steaming ordure).

Those who did would have regrets to forever haunt their waking hours. And if you were one of those oddball TV '*scientists*' who liked poking about in stools to discover what level of racist we are, you'd be forgiven for having the week off. But the final punishment from the mocking gods of olfactory was merely four seconds away. Coming into view was a £10 note, wiggling its coquettish tail like a seahorse attracting mates. With a short window of seconds to decide, this unemployed young man had a choice to make: reach into the doom and feast like a shitty-fingered king for the weekend, or leave it to the neighbouring pluckier prospective Lottery winner sat along the cavalcade, also gazing down at what misery came before. I'll leave it to your impeccable judgement to conclude what I did next. It wasn't Altamont. But personally much, much worse.

Chapter 6: In the Light

What I did love about festivals (apart from shitty fingers) was the flexible rules around bonfires, which for raging pyros known for lobbing errant butane bottles onto the beach pyre and running like fuck, was manna to our mischief. But for the most part, it was the primordial fascination of sitting around a burning stack of eye-reddening woodsmoke in a warm cwtch that countered the cooling eventide. The fields around the beer, food and comedy tents at Glasto were irradiated by small bonfires, which when viewed from the summit of the Tor, must have seemed like nomadic outposts of the Samburu. Except that instead of chewing khat, we were downing scrumpy and cracking our molars on uncooked rice. Bedouins were substituted by a nexus of stoned rockers, emaciated punks in circus mohicans (and even more comedically overlarge Docs), and hardened crusties who spent the whole summer travelling from one festival to the next in a ramshackled bus, taking full advantage of what they considered to be their right to gratis hospitality from Michael Eavis. Despite this incontrovertible precept that a huge commercial dairy farm was anathema to their principles, these plastic anarcho-levellers were never slow in coming forward if there was a free handout; meat-based capitalism or not. That's always been the problem I have with hippies. I hate them. They would shun you like you had a cholera bacillus, but would literally dine with jouissance from your outstretched palms if you had something they wanted at no cost or effort to them. Cynical breadheads encased in oversized Peruvian yak knitwear, with a dab of patchouli behind the ears to accentuate that earthy bent. At least a gang of fearsome-looking punks or huge death metalheads would invite you in and give you their last. And tidy up their shit afterwards. It must be a class thing, I suppose. Anyone named Tarquin Sky who can afford to bugger off in a huge converted bus to a yogic retreat in Deja doesn't need my charity.

Fire will bring tribes together, but not always in the spirit of cordiality. I remember gawping in stupefaction as a burly denim hairy from a biker gang, slugging from a demijohn of Somerset's crudest pressed windfall, alighted upon the neighbouring pyre of a Hare Krishna troupe, and homed in on who appeared to be the head monk. An exchange took place, whence said greasy started finger-jabbing at the beatific priest, who offered august blessings of jeu d'esprit in retort. This visibly irked the denim brigand, who became increasingly irate at any solemn and cleverclogs offerings. The discourse escalated, with Beardy screaming *"I'LL FUCKIN' KILL YOU!!"* Reaching into the fire to retrieve a thick orange-glowing log, he started swinging it violently above his head like a transgender majorette at the Highland Games, scattering the golden throng of Buddhists in a backwash of sandals, beads, and jangling finger crotales. Open-mouthed, my mate and I turned to each other and agreed to ease off on the cider for a bit.

Prometheus stole fire from the gods, but was punished for this act. Probably with a visit to the nearest burns unit and the mother of all hangovers. Local mythology has it that in the 17th century, the landlord of a Pilton pub, possibly also known as Tom the Taverner, was hanged for engaging in criminal activity. I'd like to think that he was sentenced by the local assizes in revenge for causing an outbreak of dysentery and fighting amidst holy men and cavalry following a quintal of his special pear and rat shit ferment.

The great philosopher and humanitarian Albert Schweitzer once wrote: *"In everyone's life, at some time, our inner fire goes out. It is then burst into flame by an encounter with another human being. We should all be thankful for those people who rekindle the inner spirit."* Aside from violent culture clashes framed by incense and diesel, festival fires are always the best places for gossip, stories, and mythology, all of which I find life-affirming. They open up the best in us all, the finest memories, daftest events and funniest tales. Despite all the magnificent squalor, free music, anarchy, and cheap weed, my fondest recall of a 1982 event near the fabled rock formations of Stonehenge was of a portly woman sat next to me around the hearth, piss-taking the smelly hippies and their faux cockney Jagger drawls, and providing a long, rib-crackingly funny anecdote—delivered in sardonic tones- about her horny Yorkshire Terrier who would lick himself into a frenzy and at a vinegar stroke disable him from any form of movement. To this day, I will not be told by anyone (not even herself) that this wasn't Jo Brand.

The ancients were awed by the mystical powers of fire, which ensorcelled many cultures and religions, including Zoroastrianism, Hinduism, and Fred Dinenage. Flush preppies on a year's *secondment* in Bora Bora stamp through it, promulgating its cleansing properties through OMG upspeak and frenzied selfies, while the locals smirk at the twats; and home movies will capture a drunken dad acting out his last moments on Earth with a human face, showing his dominion over the flame by throwing half a gallon of petrol over a frustratingly slow barbecue.

Around a large bonfire at a small space rock festival on some Devon farmstead, I chatted to a former Hawkwind bassist who tottered unsteadily before me. A cadaverous apparition barely encased in translucent dermis, cheeks hollower than a Walnut Whip, and sunken eye globes in sockets that looked like retreating sloes imprisoned in a rail tunnel. As we shot the breeze about bands, he tucked into his Pot Noodle, which must have seemed like a vast mediaeval banquet to his attenuated satsuma of a stomach; doubling his body mass index with every al dente forkful of maltodextrin and disodium guanylate. Slowly, his eyes closed as he lurched to his right, and like a rotten folly of playing cards, gently collapsed into the inferno. Fearing that this heroin-abraded sack of skin and sticks would go up like kindle, I sprang to the rescue, lifting him out of the conflagration with the ease of retrieving a hand towel off the bathroom floor. He stood up, looked around, and casually brushed off the ashes and assemblage of glowing embers attached to his formerly iridescent rags, before sentience kicked in, reminding himself, in that hopeless squatter cockney drawl: *"fuckin' ell, man... I need to get me some noodles. Have you got a quid?"*

Chapter 7: Miasma Generator

I once entered an arcade shop in a Norfolk town, stalactites of peeling paint hanging from its façade like a leper playing chance with an upskirting Newton. Garish, ill-matched blinds peered out from seared window frames. Masses of filled jars and ephemera beckoned me in through doors that would ensnare the unwary in their beaded hangings and invoke tinnitus with a chorus of mezzo-forte wind chiming. *Hobgoblin's Garden,* I think it was called.

The first thing that struck me was that familiar smell. The aroma from university gigs; the tang of musty halls of residence; the passing whiff of a mad woman with unkempt hair; the stink of some nihilist batik class; the pungency of old metal pans caked with the veneer of overcooked pulses The place was empty. Or so it seemed.

A feint humming sound permeated the hollow random peals as a mad woman with unkempt hair materialised from behind a stack of posters that had long given up the fight to keep their vitality and submitted to yellowing in the passing seasons. The rustling of her cheesecloth grated my teeth in approach as she fiddled with the loose arm of her spectacles. She too yellowed in the passing seasons as her sepia tint dissolved into the gauche patterns of her clothing and splayed out wildly into warped, angular fingers of greying hair. The sense to recoil was strong, but like a forthcoming yawn when in delicate company, in time one develops the strength of will to beat it down. She loomed towards me, her framed eyes bulging like globes herniating from a cannibal lampshade, and stopped momentarily to elevate her sandalled foot and vigorously fondle a shedding fungal nail disorder.

By this time, the recoil had surrendered to the welling desire to flee. Yet there was a homely, reassuring quality to her. A sense that you could leave your dying, incontinent dog and return to see her covered in liquid canine ordure, retaining that faraway buoyancy and otherworldly wryness. You could visualise her droning softly while tending to a limpid cactus.

"Hi, is there anything I can help you with?" came the words, trapped in the Doppler effect of a passing gnat's ambulance. I'd only entered the shop out of inquisitiveness at seeing a stuffed kitten in a jar playing a kazoo and a hat shaped out of an armadillo. *"Well, I, er, was just, er, looking around and...* Trailing off with little conviction, I had involuntarily left the conversational door ajar, allowing her to wedge her sandalled hoof into the gap. *"Well, you look like you're into music,"* came the retort as she craned forward, spying my disintegrating Led Zeppelin t-shirt. *Into music?* What the fuck did that mean? Did I have some caterwauling seraph hovering above my head? My face is admittedly shaped like a plectrum. Perhaps like Robert Johnson, all those Delta decades ago, I had the essence of a hellhound on my tail.

Her observation reminded me of that awkward moment when my nan thought that I would like to take ownership of her clapped faux-walnut cabinet the size of a wrestler's coffin that cunningly concealed a radiogram... just because I was *into music.*

With a multi-speed, semi-circular sweep of her hand, she beckoned my attention towards a haphazard row of vinyl squashed between some hand-painted bras from Bolivia and an ashtray hewn from the scrotum of an Inuit. "*Have a look in there. See what takes your fancy.*" I observed a string of spittle forming a fragile bridge between her electrified lips. As with all vinyl junkies, second invitations are as superfluous as a nosebleed in an abattoir. I swept aside the objet d'art and, using the unique dexterity evolved from years of browsing, fingered through the stack with clockwork gusto.

It was mostly 70s tat. James Last, redundant effects albums (featuring church bells, cars, and wildlife to herald '*the superb modern wonder of stereophonic sound*'), trashy Hawaiian guitar adaptations of Beatles hits of the day (complete with suitable sunset sleeve art to enhance the exotica), and Mrs. Mills displaying her ample traits as the original party animal. All were probably considered relevant and innovative for the time, but like a Vesta curry, now languishing in a distant memory cupboard marked '*tasteless shit,*

Nostrils flared, and I felt that familiar thread of dissatisfaction starting to writhe in my stomach. I always get this when leafing through vinyl collections. So much so that it is assured to have a dysenteric effect every time. If ever I needed urgent colonic investigations for IBS, I could save the NHS a few quid on chemical bowel preparations. All I'd require is a nurse wheeling in a rack of old albums to thumb through, and hey presto: gravy time.

So, there I was rummaging through 12" purgatory and needing a dump, when I came across a lavish-looking platter with a 4-page coloured gatefold sleeve, presumably designed by one of those *visionary* album painters (Roger Dean, Rodney Matthews, etc. spring to mind) that influenced sixth-form art students to paint their common rooms in garish hues featuring nymphs on giant misshapen cock fungi. The album was called *"Seven Caves to the Ice Palace"* by Icarus Children. There is an obvious formula to this that runs as naturally as alpine cascades and can only be detected on the radar of old musos. You could wager your left kidney that it would (a) feature ex-university chums; (b) have band members called Nigel or Tony; and (c) consist of cleverclogs prog meandering, where half-way through the overlong concept based on some obscure Pratchett fable, the music would degenerate into a free-for-all of accapella sea-shantyism and pointless flute parping. Great stuff, I reckon.

But I digress. As I picked up the thick card cover and perused the gatefold, I looked closely at the band photos. These contrived snaps will always give you an idea of the type of music therein: moody youths chewing and leaning against lampposts will usually gob out an image of punk; sneering moustached men surrounded by the paraphernalia of Satanism, yet preening through flowing blow-dried locks, would suggest cod heavy metal; sepia-tinted confederate mock-ups always conspire to exhibit the worst type of country rock; and in this case, a cabal of eccentrics, including a balding professor-type holding up a cor anglais with a gnome peeking out of the end; a lanky man in gaudy tank-top trying to look bemused; and a bespectacled woman in a kaftan, wild fingers of greying hair...

Hold on. Rewind. I did one of those Oliver Hardy double-takes and swallowed hard. To complete the set, all I needed was to step back into a large bucket of paint and receive a loose shelving unit full of large tins in my face. I rubbed my eyes and looked again. It couldn't be. As I pondered such things, I felt a waft of moist, foetid breath on my nape. *"Yes, that's me,"* came the voice, and I turned to view a chilling rictus replete with bulging eyes as she jabbed her finger towards the sleeve in a staccato rhythm as if trying to punch a hole into worlds beyond. Rooted to the spot, a gurgling mash of vowels tripped from my lips as my focus came to and fro between the photo and the shopkeeper. *"I played the hurdy gurdy and fingerbells on most of the tracks. We were considered to be the next big thing in Norfolk and Suffolk, and once supported Steeleye Span at the Ipswich Gaumont. Hahahaha!!"*. I dropped the album and ran out of the shop, trailing air croutons and gasping in fear. I tore down the road, powered with adrenaline, at the pace of a relay anchorman with a ralgexed arsehole.

Years later, I drove through the same town and hung a left into the street of *'Hobgoblin's Garden'*. It had been replaced by a charity shop for spastic donkeys. I was urged to look inside out of devilment to see if a whiff of traumas past would hang in the air. It was mostly run by old jam-mongers and middle-class teaching assistants, and had that familiar sense of order interspersed with chaos that one gets in a charity shop. However, I spied something familiar. It was a stuffed kitten in a jar playing a kazoo, with a price tag of £3 attached to it. As I reached in awe, a crinkled whisper hanging in the umbra behind me broke the bustle: "*You look like you're into music....*"

Chapter 8: Suey Seems To Be The Hardest Word

What is it about the late-night dining experience that brings out the basest instincts of humanity's dreg-scraping animus? More often than not, we'd quietly flat-line through the day, disturbing neither hide nor hair in custom and tradition. Saying sorry to random strangers we may impede as they travel along their own neural pathways. However, pollute our systems with nocturnal alcohol, head off for a curry, and we suddenly turn into an overbearing invasion of obnoxious commentary, foul table manners, and xenophobic disrespect for those employed to cook, not to mention those inclined to eat alongside us. How many of us have ever, in a state of sobriety and tucking into our midnight concoctions, laughed, shook our heads, or wanted to throw a punch as some inebriated, inflated braggart entered the dining room and started bellowing, *"Oi, Ghandi; I'll have a big fuckoff alsation khorma, pronto!"* ?

Like football hooliganism, the perplexing way that this behaviour is somewhat considered reputable and acceptable as a *'badge'* of alpha masculinity in Britain tells us a lot about the society we live in. We curl back in revulsion when a piss-reeking tramp waves a can of thrift store cider in our faces. We look the other way and tut (or even film on our phones) when someone staggers on the bus and whines a tirade of religious tongues while pointing menacingly at their own reflection. Yet somehow we let it slide quietly when an intoxicated tattooed homunculus, with his belly flopping out of an open shirt stained with dribble and emesis, hurls racist jibes at oriental food servants.

I must ashamedly admit to once being part of cuisine terrorism in such a place. In fact, I should say that the night in question was of such low etiquette anarchy that I should rightly be hogtied and carted off to have my head immersed in the used disposal chute of a busy tandoori kitchen.

The venue in question was The Dragon Chop Suey House, an old, established Chinese eatery in the main part of town. Despite tastes becoming more sophisticated as we embraced multiculturalism in the dying embers of the 20th century, the *'Dragon'* remained steadfast against the advancing army of Cantonese fare; offering staple choices, including chips with eyes glowing in thyroid stares and a prawn curry that looked like the end product of a home abortion kit. The ambience was of traditional Mandarin folk harmony that hung in the foetid air lit by flickering yellow light bulbs before running down the peeling flock wallpaper and gasping its last breath prone on stained crimson rubber tablecloths. I swear that one of those cloths bore my name, drunkenly engraved by a fork at least three years previously.

Every town has events that, while memorable, become embellished to the point of legend in subsequent shakedown. Example: A simple scuffle outside a kebab house becomes the stuff of cinematic Kurosawa battles across widescreen urban planes involving sophisticated weaponry, arson of properties, and a police tactical response unit supported by attack helicopters. This particular night at The Dragon was no exception. I'll lead you to believe.

I was part of a group of seven (which included a dwarf, a Tourette's sufferer, and a heavily inked, permanently pissed skinhead) that descended upon The Dragon in order to replenish the monosodium glutamate diluted by a night of dense alcoholic osmosis. I suppose, given the skinhead reference, we could pay tribute to Yul Brynner and call ourselves *The Municipal Seven.*

Anyway, picture the scene: a septet of boorish drunken freaks enters a packed restaurant to find only one table for four available. Those swift of foot grabbed the opportunity in a tottering haphazardness akin to musical chairs on a North Sea fishing vessel. Those left behind would have to embrace the fusty purgatory of the upstairs *'overflow'* room. I found myself in the former group. Nosferatu and Tattoo (to use crude descriptive noms de guerre for the skinhead and dwarf, respectively) were sentenced to the latter. So far, so good. I hear you mumble at this juncture.

The problem is that The Dragon employed some of the most belligerent and rude waiters west of the Silk

Road (understandable I guess, given their abuse at the hands of filthy clientele down the ages), including the owner, the diminutive Mr. Hong, who sauntered around in a frayed tuxedo topped by a comical ill-fitting acrylic toupee. In the lexicon of local witticism, it came as no surprise that he was universally known as *'Wiggy'*. He always kept the same furrowed-brow expression, and his sucking lemon mouth puckered like a little cat's arse. Hong and those in his employ barked out rapid fire discourse conditioned from years of Sinophobia. *"You order food!"*. *"No drink beer 'til you order food..."* and so on. This didn't help matters on a night that was starting to turn sweet and sour. Without the sweet.

No sooner had we sat down than a squeal filled the foetid air. *"You steal knife and fork!"*. One of the waiters had insisted—incorrectly, by the way—that he'd laid the table and we'd half-inched the Wiggy family silver. Soon we were surrounded by minuscule men in black waistcoats, pecking at us in cartoon Jackie Chan voices to *"give back knife fork! Give back knife and fork!"*. The problem is, Alan Tourette's was at our table. The most crudely cynical man in Celtic lore. *"Fuck, fuck, fuck, fuck, fuck, fuuuuuck that!"* came the admeasured retort like an idling truck with a fractured exhaust. With that, we were *'invited'* to turn out our pockets to prove our innocence of such a heinous felony. Readers: look away now.

"Up my fuckin' arsehole!" came the rejoinder as Mr Tourette's clambered up onto the table and commenced disrobing. The rest of us provided a soundtrack via the famous 1958 David Rose tune *'The Stripper'* (*Da da daaa, dada da daaa,* if that's any help at all). Emboldened by the discordant choir and unison table drumming of all punters present, off came the shirt and trousers. Mouldy socks were given the twirly finger tassel treatment before being catapulted across the room, presumably into some unfortunate's Bombay Duck. As the diners continued joining in with a crescendo of noise, and just as the ill-fitting y-fronts were about to be peeled south, Wiggy screamed: *"You stop! Get dressed! No clothes! No knife or fork! No food!"*

Unwittingly, in attempting to prove our innocence in the dark underworld of cutlery crime, we'd broken urban rule No. 1: never misbehave before the meal arrives. Otherwise, a) it'll not get delivered, or b) it will have the chef's salivary (or other) emissions mixed in with the sauce. Anyway, Wiggy, bruised by the impromptu lap dance and the realisation that his waiter was indeed an idiot, started to push and prod. *"You get out! You trouble! No food! No food!"* He was clearly distracted as the next event unfolded.

Punters began complaining that something was dripping onto their heads and plates from the ceiling above. Wiggy dispatched a minion to investigate upstairs, fearing a burst water main. Suddenly a high-pitched *"Noooooo!!!"* echoed down the flight as everyone stopped eating out of curiosity. Had the giant tank of ornamental carp burst its glass banks? The situation was much worse, as an ashen waiter threw himself down the stairs, fell at the last two steps, and staggering on his knees, grabbed at Wiggy's cummerbund, gasping: *"Bald man, bald man, bald man, pass water...."*

Consider for one minute the potential for savage dismemberment here. I'm not talking about the average kicking, but the planned use of rendering skills by Shaolin chefs with jagged kitchen implements. The solution was to act fast to save our follicle-challenged bladder exhibitionist on the first floor. Wiggy was in the throes of yelling an adjure to his kitchen assassins (and if you've tasted the food, you'll respect this as a valid description), and we were poised to produce a deft strategy of containment, when a completely random punter appeared from the bamboo shadows and snatched off Wiggy's hairpiece, before racing out the door and down Station Road, waving his prize triumphantly like someone who'd just thumped in the cup final winner. There was momentary silence followed by a huge uproar of mirth, which swept across The Dragon like a cloud of sarin gas. Ovation and table-banging ensued as women fell off their chairs in mascara-coated delirium. Men, doubled up in tears, attempted to stop their floating ribs from convulsing Alien-like through abdominal cavities of glee.

Wiggy's expression was akin to that of a Sunday school teacher who'd just discovered porno mags amidst the tambourines. In what seemed like only seconds, yet probably thought decades for the Wigmeister, he fumbled through the coat racks and grabbed his trusty old pork pie hat, donning it quickly as if it was full of priceless liquid & polystyrene bits. We all have this inexplicable trait of doing something –anything- to cover up an embarrassing situation, despite everyone and his bloody dog seeing it. Example: how many of us have had our feet up on the desk at work only for the boss to walk in, resulting in us sharply swinging them down? How many times have we pretended we haven't fallen or badly twisted our ankle, despite a whole precinct of people witnessing it & wincing through their teeth? This assumes that everyone but ourselves spark into an amnesiac catalepsy whenever events befall, allowing us to escape, dignity intact. This of course was Wiggy's rationale: basically, we hadn't noticed that the old fucker was balder than a terrapin's scrotum because we were too preoccupied with piss dripping on our heads. Thankfully, the toupee thief had delayed the inevitable carnage.

Well, not quite. There was still an incontinent skinhead to deal with. Three waiters, mummified with cloths, and Mrs Wiggy, armed with a broom ascended the stairs with trepidation at the watery funeral that awaited. The earlier frivolity had subsided to a grave hush, which was akin to a Leone western climax as chimes, jangling guitars and close-ups of nervous twitchy faces -eyes darting from left to right- heralded the inevitable denouement. Metaphorical buzzards circled overhead and tumbleweeds billowed across plates of uneaten chop suey. Suddenly it erupted. A crash, followed by *"fuck you!!"* as Nosferatu came tumbling into the stairwell, his jeans matted with urine and Mrs Wiggy lunging behind, wielding a spinning brush like a psychotic majorette. Who can underestimate the incredible bravery of a pocket-sized lady against a six foot hairless oik who'd just relieved himself over her customers? A few more whacks with the broom and he was out through the door and into the gutter outside, half-laughing, half-agonising. She turned to us, our faces ashen. *"Now yooo get fucky out my restaurant!!"*. We slowly rose in unison, our gazes shifting side to side to each other and back to the armed banshee about to do us some triad damage. Time to leave. Quietly. While we still had fingers.

Just then, another aberrant noise erupted from the top of the stairs. *"bllooooaaar!! I'm gonna be sick!!!….."* Tattoo, our stunted friend had obviously become too tired & emotional, and the heady cocktail of beers & chasers had finally pushed his equilibrium above the plimsole line of containment. We looked up to see Neil (the hitherto unmentioned member of our troupe) carrying Tattoo under his arm, staggering down the stairs while the latter vomited over the side of the banister. Try to imagine someone walking off with a ventriloquist's dummy that's suddenly losing its innards and you'll be half-way there to the scene now being played in your mind. Needless to say, the place was no longer in uproarious mood. There was an almost psychedelic solemnity of awe. As if one had just witnessed the passing of a UFO with Rod Hull on a bungee.

At this stage it was clear that the proprietors had lost the will to live. Wiggy was waving and gesticulating like a points duty official who'd just discovered drum & bass; the waiters were propping each other up in obfuscation and mental exhaustion, and Mrs Wiggy was using the broom to scoop up the lumps of dwarf chunder that had rebounded off walls and light fittings. There was a sense of bewilderment and fear of the sort that you'd see in the faces of working-class kids given tickets to *Waiting for Godot*.

But why spoil the good night without a climax? Exultantly, Mr Tourette's shouted: *"Runner!!"*, and with that we took off towards the door. Urban rule no.2: when someone shouts *"Runner!"* you have no option but to surf the wave of rapid exit strategy or otherwise you'll be saddled with paying for a meal for seven (that was never delivered) just to cover the chaos and reputational damage. It's wrong, but I'll be fucked if I'm going to cough up because of someone else's moral compass that was more diseased than my own.

So out we surged, hopefully content in the knowledge that Wiggy & co. were too strung out to even care by now. Unfortunately, Tourette's decided that a more decorative exit would be appropriate, and grabbed the sheets of three tables as he run past, dragging everyone's meals in a huge slipstream of noodles & hoi sin. As we got to the door, we couldn't flip the bloody latch. This is a typical example of how panic can render the easiest tasks impossible (try operating your seat belt or opening a childproof paracetamol bottle when you're in a rush). As we shanked at the hitherto unsophisticated Yale locking mechanism, I peered back into the restaurant to see several kitchen staff tearing out at pace, holding bamboos that were as thick as my arm. *"Gerra fuckin move on!!!"* shouted Tourette's, holding stained tablecloths like he'd just nicked the Turin Shroud. We managed to open it and burst out into the street, running like the wind (or maybe gambolling unsteadily like a haphazard zephyr) pursued by screaming chinamen waving the deadly implements of our demise. Combat tactics always suggest throwing hunters off your trail by splitting up. Deciding this was the best policy I broke away from the peloton and headed down a back lane. Unfortunately, the punishers decided to take my scent. 100 yards into urban darkness and I could not run any more. Adrenaline is a fast-burning chemical that lays waste to energy over a short period, leaving a shell fuelled purely by alcohol. Basically, I was shagged out. They were upon me.

Rather than put up a fight and get a large hollow stick across my beautiful face, I determined that the best policy would be to drop & roll, and curl up into a foetal position. As I hit the damp tarmac corrupted by domestic waste, syringe wrappers & old men's snot, I was surrounded by four oriental enforcers, who decided to beat seven colours of shit out of me as if they were putting out a small forest fire. Wave upon wave of wretchedness arrived. Then nothing. They had disappeared into the night with the contents of my wallet. The only ambience was a feint ringing in my ears providing a soundtrack to the searing pain across my arms, legs and torso.

Eventually I was reunited with my group, who staggered in astonishment at the welts from a painful retribution. Some laughed, and I laughed with them, no matter how much it hurt. Someone said: *"Anyone fancy a kebab?"*

Chapter 9: Beached

Childhood can sketch memories that race from the cloaked corridors of the psyche to the forefront of your thoughts with the random unpredictability of an old drunk in a bus shelter. You could be sitting on a deckchair, and a distant waft of something will bring back a picture of time and place. Your first fight; your first kiss; or even the time you got lost, and as the sun started its descent, the fear that you might never make it home for toast and tea. Your heart starts to race, and you could almost be in that place again.

Whoever could associate Tesco with such powerful childhood memories? The corporate bastards have crushed any sense of community under their relentless jackboot. I hate the smugness of their commercials, and a bolus of vomit rises whenever I see customers in a zombified stupor at the self-service checkouts, without realising the implications of it for the people who work and shop there. Yet I cannot stay away because of one specific reason: memories of happier times. And it's all to do with the fish counter.

Psychologists have long recognised the link between olfactory senses and memory: cut grass, burning wood, brand new plastic footballs, the rain on summer tarmac, a dead Sparrow I chased the girls in the yard with, etc. But the bloody fish counter in Tesco? This has its origins in a memorable summer spent at Morfa Beach in the days when 10-year-olds were allowed to wander for miles in the wilderness, unshackled by parental fears of predatory nomads and free from the threat of an ASBO. Older generations will always spout on at increasing revisionist length about how all summers were long and hot. And I'll be buggered if I'm going to disagree.

This particular season seems etched into my brain with a solar stencil. They may very well have been different summers, but to assist the embellishing of reminiscence when I'm finally chained to a commode dribbling a mulch of bread from the corner of my abusive contorted mouth that angrily bites the forearm of a nurse, I will put it in one pigeonhole: summer 1973. A million UV-scorched events: getting bitten by an adder; being chased by a vagrant we caught wanking in a shed; climbing the ropes of a huge empty circus marquee; getting a sly glimpse of 14-year-old Sharon's ample breasts; making dens in haystacks; building tree swings that would propel you perilously through small forest fires. And a dead whale on the beach.

The latter scene featured an unfortunate creature who had presumably found its sophisticated sonar corrupted by a local sargasso of industrial crude, used condoms, and domestic sewage and stranded itself on the deserted beaches behind the steelworks. Word soon got around, and an army of delirious locals headed in rabid anticipation to the rare sight like attending a public hanging. The only thing is that we got there first. Nothing could beat a Raleigh Chopper propelled across sandy terrain by excited schoolkids.

Our imaginations spiralled with visions of a giant leviathan that would swallow the town whole—a maritime monster with the souls of lost seafarers imprisoned in its belly. Reality was a 12-foot pilot whale in an early state of decomposition being picked at by seagulls like some mouldering smorgasbord. Of course, the seeping oils and liquefying blubber didn't put off a load of panting kids who couldn't believe the sight before them. We clambered over the demised demon, slid down its brow, used its tail as a trampoline, and attempted the Fosbury Flop over its collapsing spine and into the sand pools formed by its once-thrashing bulk. Meanwhile, the summer sun was calling in its debt and turning the poor bastard green. A noxious aroma curled at our noses and concocted pits of nausea, calling out for the reflex of gag. The novelty was beginning to drop off like the barnacles that had accompanied the beast on many Atlantic journeys. And the adults were coming, with their earnest faces of disapproval.

I took one look back and realised there was one area we hadn't yet exploited for our novelty. We couldn't get at the teeth, and the gulls had harvested its eyes. Armed with a pointed piece of driftwood, I jumped onto its back and, with an *"Arrrrrr!!"* like the best pantomime Blackbeard, plunged the stick deep into its spout. A sickly squelch of sodomy echoed from its midst. Removing the shank, I bent forward to view the aperture and was showered in a vast geyser of putrid mammalian lung water. It was the smell of death. The stench of a piscine holocaust. I started to vomit, and those close by who were splashed with the spittle of beached doom also started retching. But we were laughing. Laughing at the stupidity, the idiocy, and the karma of disrespecting one of God's great and gentle creatures. We were covered in cadaverous stagnation, and we didn't give a fuck.

It took days to get rid of that acrid stink. Dozens of baths and clothes changes. I can still smell the putrefaction to this day. Curiously, it's a reassuring smell. A smell that tells of better times of no worry, no pressure, and no responsibility. And sometimes this smell comes to me at the Tesco fish counter. Almost beckoning me to leap into the midst of dead wall-eyed swimmers and crushed ice, plunging a great stick into the void and heading back to the summer of 1973.

It Came from Beneath the Sea

With a ham-hocked visage
And sequacious badinage
It had to be a mirage
Volute to you and me
It came from beneath the sea.

A legume of distaste
Made in cut and paste
From the moods of commonplace
Heaved ashore in brusquely
It came from beneath the sea.

Foretold in sacred text
Doomsday tellers craned their necks
Panic shoppers filled their kecks
In a screaming reverie
It came from beneath the sea.

Fleeing climbers kicked their crampons
Skinheads found a dog to stamp on
A pulsing nest of used tampons
Engulfed the coterie
It came from beneath the sea.

Puzzled generals did gird their loins
A militia crowdfund of bitcoins
From Aberavon to Des Moines
Razed the bourgeoisie
It came from beneath the sea.

You can quantify the facts
In ceremonies you can't enact
But how do you react
To an organic bestiary
That came from beneath the sea?

Chapter 10: Pit and the Pendulum

It's a strange feeling to view the foaming wave of misplaced nostalgia from those who seek evocation of the 80s like some brain-perverting smell from last year's grass cuttings where we buried the cat. These nobodies, who wish they were somebodies again, feed flesh to the parasites of a decades-dead culture in the hope of the fattened juices once again oozing out to shrivel our tongues in rancidity at the return of singing Page 3 girls, shoulder pads, yuppies, Tories, and, worse, Duran fucking Duran.

The 1980s smeared a shimmering veneer on the dark infestations bubbling rancorously beneath UK's society. While people in outlandish quiffs and thick red braces called Balthasar or Crispin bellowed into their crate-sized mobile phones, others endured years of unimaginable struggle and hardship, doomed to be picked off by the auguries of their demise, like harpies at a KFC trolley dash.

My dad was such a victim. His career as a crane driver at Port Talbot steelworks smashed against the rocks of *'competitiveness'*; his security and career definition were thrown onto a putrescent heap containing all his school friends, followed by a liberal sprinkling of management quicklime and spittle from a traitorous steel union and Labour Party to dull the rancour. I can still picture him wandering in the garden, shuffling aimlessly in a soporific daze of disbelief, when he learned that he was going to be made redundant. While never displaying anything of the militancy of some of his striking cohorts, he nevertheless was enraged enough to enlist on the picket lines, and emboldened by this unnatural rush of comradeship, kicked down the door of the fearfully abandoned payroll office. I don't know if he expected to find anything other than meaningless reams of printouts, discarded fag coupons, and a saucy calendar, but he'll never convince anyone that it wasn't he who curled one out on the cashier manager's desk.

The dismantling of the public steel industry by Thatcher and her chosen executioner, MacGregor, was akin to Victorian surgeons peeling at a wretched disparate strapped to a gurney, scything with aplomb at the flesh, and leaving behind a blob of writhing scabrous mulch that would implode in its own gangrenous gases. Thousands suddenly found themselves without a future, and although sales of Betamax video recorders hit critical mass, so did the sight of grown men drunkenly staggering out of social clubs, their thousand-yard stares framed in bloodshot eyes of bleakness. Fists clenched to either dab at these new tears or break the teeth of any infidel who dared suggest they were living it large.

Taking on the steel workers was Thatcher's little dress rehearsal for the miners. Like a precocious debutante about to perform at the local village hall, trying out her talent on a front room of squeaking, pissing grannies too demented or timid to denounce the nauseating circus of delusion before them.

Eulogised by the Sun-reading masses only too keen to devour spurious pictures amidst the tits of a UK pauperised by unburied dead children and sneering blackened faces sticking their unwashed cocks into screen-printed flags of the Queen, Thatcher drew a line in the coal where uniforms and riot shields assembled to beat a rhythmic Zulu cant before staving in the skulls of men trying to save their jobs and the heartbeat of their communities. 1984: The last great battle for the soul of Britain's society had begun, and things would never be the same again.

Consider for one moment two conflicting ideologues, stripped bare and ready for rumpus, like a brace of rancorous oafs in a pub, building disagreements, bubbling hostility, and pumping facile gesticulation. In the blue corner, we had a paid army of the profiteering elite, gill-stuffed with inherited sweetmeats and pampered with rivers of jus pouring from their sweat ducts. In the red corner, we got hard men of the soil— coal-tattooed broken skin spawned from forebears of struggle, hacking at apertures inside mountains. Carving out sunlight-impenetrable arteries. Choked off from the rest of the world, their families and communities must have seemed like arcane remote tribes to the swaggering hedge fund yahoos of the age who gambled the fruits of our labours.

Thatcher's desire to smash the NUM heralded pathways to one of the most noxiously sorrowful sagas of social cleansing this country has ever had the horror to stand by and do fuck all about. Transforming mining communities into alcohol-ravaged Aboriginal wastelands of despair meant little to those who lubricated the itchy palms of finance and elevated further the plutocracy of the inherited. One wonders how the *'grocer's daughter'* would have reacted if the police turned up in full riot gear to shut down her dad's business, threatening to seize his assets and stamp on his face if he so much as *looked at them in a funny way*. How would the latter-day *St. Francis of Assisi* eke out a daily skirmish of snagged leggings in needle-strewn, faeces-painted tenements, every essence of opportunity and hope submerged in the blackened waters of spite? I'm sure she would have said a little prayer for that enterprise zone that popped up on scrub land. A large corrugated outhouse in pastel colours trying to teach modern office skills to men who couldn't even hold a fucking pen due to vibration in their white fingers, let alone learn the art of creative CV writing.

All wars start off like two drunken pugilists in a pub, followed by inevitable clashes that usually involve others; recruiting allies more skilled in the martial ways of delivering a kick; and getting everyone around to side with them in the belief that they hold the moral high ground. Arthur Scargill, the belligerent humourless NUM leader responded to having a metaphorical pint tipped over him, warning everyone that the Tories were shutting down pits and killing livelihoods simply out of spite and a desire to dissolve the powerful adhesive holding together workers' rights: the NUM. Ah, yes, the NUM. That monster of discontent, threshing against the progressing tides. As the tabloids would have you believe.

Thatcher, buoyed by prevailing over the steel and rail workers with the embarrassing ease of holding a small child by the head at arm's length and chortling as it swung air punches and a bosom lactating with notches of the Belgrano dead, brought in some *outside help* in the form of migrant enforcers MacGregor (who had already warmed-up by taking on the steelworkers, and Murdoch. The former ripped out teeth with brutal pliers, the latter telling terrified onlookers that *"it was done for their own good"*. Violent protection racketeering with old men's masks replacing stockings or Halloween faces. If they were *Sweeney* villains, they would be crackly-spoken basement strip club owners in Foster Grant shades and plaid slacks, grinning mordantly as they puffed a Monte Cristo the size of a table leg and fondled a large Martini in a gold sovereign and monogrammed bracelet-choked hand that had earlier strangled a greyhound.

While the media and the ubiquitous assortment of have-bilge-will-travel and pun-for-hire modern historians were desirous to embellish a canvas of civil war between the miners and the police, it was not

Orgreave here. For many at the local front end, most days were predominantly spent in the embrace of amorphous boredom, where a skeleton crew of pickets were shadowed at the entrance to Port Talbot steelworks by an equally nonplussed chorus line of well-upholstered town constabulary. Residents and journalists scratched their heads at the curious and perversely heartwarming spectacle of supposed sworn enemies utilising the public green to sunbathe, gossip, share crossword clues, and enjoy the sort of simplistic cricket matches with flexible rules that would encumber the patience gland of any Wisden pedant.

Thus, we had '*Pigs VI vs. Enemy Within VII*' in *The Strike Ashes*. As fitting for such juvenile pursuits, the analogous jumpers for goalposts were supplanted by a wicket tower of police helmets, looking eerily akin to a dwarf minaret of vanquished Aztec skulls. The bewildered gazes of locals were fed by the spectacle of what was happening at the crease: leg swingers jettisoned with prejudice from the giant hands of a collier and met brutally by a uniformed enforcer waving a cudgel of fake willow. Jovial sledging from extra cover, as a distant harmonica refrain of the theme tune from '*Dixon of Dock Green*' emanated amidst the discordant rasps of coal-baked lung from mid-off.

A neighbour emerged with a jug of lemonade the size of a fish tank for the cops and a selection of ciders and lagers for the drooling miners. Emboldened by fluid, one of the constables attempted a mighty six over the nearby A48. Tracking the ball's trajectory on descent, *Harmonica* raced onto the highway, oblivious to midday traffic, and into the path of an oncoming freight truck. Everyone clenched their buttocks and averted their gazes from the denouement, just like we do when channel surfing horror porn. We waited amidst the resounding screech of brakes and hung fearfully upon the inevitability of that sickening bump of metal against bone and flesh. It never happened. Silence.

Slowly, through the haze of tyre smoke and dust devils, came the coughed refrain of *'Dixon of Dock Green'*, as our hero emerged out of the haze holding the catch above his head. Between mouth organ breaths, shouting: *"Out! Ya fuckin' pig bastard!"* and everyone sank to the ground as if kneecapped by the machine guns of merriment. Think of that scene the next time you watch *'Once Upon a Time in the West— and* imagine Charles Bronson in Edgbaston whites, tripping over a pigeon as Jack Elam laughs his good eye out.

But such acts reside in the pleasure zones of memory. Like I said, events were mostly great swathes of tedium yielding to the odd, exciting episode like sitting on the river's edge and waiting for the re-emergence of a Kingfisher. Thus we had the above, with a pentameter of skirmish > disquiet > calm > disquiet > skirmish, and sometimes all-out combat. Maybe that's how wars are, where the downtime feeds the senses and kneads the suspense. Hardly Hitchcock, but if I were commissioned to make a film of the strike, it would for the most part consist of stocky men recumbent on deckchairs waiting for the call-to-arms; close-up shots of increasing sweat beads as the distant rumble of a few coal lorries got louder and nearer. And they'd crack open another beer and say *"fuck it. Can't be arsed today."*

Even before the advent of mobile phones, one could get word of an approaching coal convoy: a hundred or so lorries powered on the fumes of unfettered abuse from drivers shepherded through to the works' ore terminal, where imported coking coal from South Africa and Chile (with the compliments of Thatcher's altruistic bedfellows, Botha and Pinochet) would be transported to Aberthaw power station, 50 miles east. The irony of keeping the nation's lights on, while mining villages were having theirs snuffed out. Divisions of police would appear mysteriously, like rogue tides that trap you on a causeway. Legions of miners would emerge, seemingly from pores in the Earth. Both sides would take up positions. In a tacit nod to the rules of engagement, as the convoy passed through, there would be a well-rehearsed training scrum of push and counter-push to the soundtrack of *'Scab!!'* Nobody got hurt. Nobody got arrested. Not a single stone was thrown. Not a single skull broken with batons. Robust protesting countered by restrained enforcement, followed by lull, dissolve, and back to the deckchairs and beer. Almost like an annual over-40s charity rugby match, but with fake scowls. Apart from one weekend, when it all went so horribly wrong.

More about that later. But this is the paradox, the confusion. Bewilderment broiled in the essence of ambiguity and waterboarded in a cryptogram gumbo. What you get when attempting to fathom the unfathomable pointlessness of Cluedo with equally befuddled relatives in those interminable yuletide shindigs where Uncle Michael would stand over you with another offering of rum that seemingly had been fermenting in the airing cupboard since 1967 and Nana would keep lifting up her skirt to the shrill of septuagenarian whooping while dropping her top set, which would be filched and taken to the secret lair of a clepto border collie. The lost days before YouTube. How the fuck did we all survive?

The miners must have felt this. A nimbus of wretchedness ascending out of your gut with each day minus a wage. Every hour spent away from your wife and kids as eyes broil with saline reverie of them sustained by the kindness of others. It was your job to put food on the table or gifts at their feet. Tucking into your dog-eared sleeping bag in a dank makeshift quarterage while cops on treble time payments and hauliers with fat bonuses tucked into thick quilts weighted down by a myriad of strewn holiday brochures and appended the cruelty by waving their pay packets at you. *What is wrong with you?*

Everything you fought for was milled into the sodden earth of lies by a cadre of Tory media, a nosegay-holding establishment, and vacillating poltroons from the Labour Movement who didn't step up and shield you when it mattered. The name *'Kinnock'* is an etched verb for *'sneaky shit'* in south Wales, e.g., *"Just nipping to the bogs for a Kinnock."*

How do we abstract this? Where do we take it? To what deity can we drag our mangled souls for redemption? How can we look in the mirror at the vague shape who was masticated brutally, projectile spat, set aflame and stamped upon, dragged across broken Jars where hearts and butterflies were once kept? That ashen visage points back in mocking contempt. We hardly recognise it, but from inside we can hear the echoes of our former selves laughing and singing—like we did when we were invincible. The raven scars remain tattooed on faces as a covenant to those who stood up to be counted but ended on their knees as the discounted. At least we can be content that some miners may still have enough bladder function in their dying days to be able to piss on Thatcher's grave and watch the steam rise from the Hellion cage she would writhe in for eternity.

Lull and action. Withdraw. Lull and action. Withdraw. Isn't this the music of war? A big swelling pustule of boredom lanced by a discordant kick in the ear? Bit like a Clash album I suppose (well, I can't keep picking on Uriah Heep all the time). If Orgreave was the *Mother of All Battles*, then the *Great Skirmish of Margam* was more like a dust-up outside Greggs. So it came to pass. The cricket gear was locked away. The big hard boys were coming to town to stamp on our sandcastles. Army cosplay in unmarked uniforms. No cavalry, just the ambient miners choir raising the ghosts of Calvary.

Stiffening sinews and girding loins, captained on a muscular journey by cramping arthritis from the blackening legacy of damp tunnels and freezing air shafts. Dermal self-basting in the dampness of a south Wales solstice. Relief finds passages through camaraderie and beer. Always beer. A throat lacerated by minute daggers of anthracite will always self-medicate with beer. After all is done, and after everything was ending; who was going to deny them this one final pleasure?

But back to the skirmish.

Well, as a digression; one other final picture. In a previous chapter I wrote about drugs, and in particular, our old pal the magic mushroom. They grew in abundance on the hills around, living cheek-by-jowl with kilos of the traditional breakfast variant. I knew the best fields and yields. Every year I'd be staggering down mountain paths with half my body weight in bags of common fungi acting as decoy for the cache of mind-warping contraband secluded underneath. Sometimes the miners would come up to the ridge with me, sometimes I would be their delivery boy. For the most-part it was breakfast supplements to their eggs & bacon, with a little sprinkling of caps on the side. Over the weeks, the fungal ratio would switch, and you could hear them laughing heartily from their cabin well into the night.

But back to the skirmish (*get on with it – Ed*).

Mythology and lore is for the most part based on local perceptions and exaggerations of key events. Thus, the late-night drunk trying to find his way home across an unlit field becomes a fugitive prowler checking on the shallow graves of his vanished family (rather than them all pissing off years ago to a new life away from the inebriated loser who chopped down his stairs for firewood). Stories stretch the imagination to hitherto unimaginable levels of credulity.

The miners' picket of Port Talbot had its own stories of local spies paid for by the government to keep tabs on the comings and goings at the strikers' portakabin; special forces army placements amidst the police to act as agitators; the police themselves arresting anyone who dared to breathe within 100 yds of the protests on trumped-up charges (I was stopped on three occasions for a *'bicycle check'*, and charged with faulty brakes. Every time I used the alias Robert Wyatt, and a fictitious address, knowing full well that the members of our constabulary would never have heard of the erstwhile Soft Machine drummer and Canterbury indie legend, or be arsed to check if I lived there). There was a sense of bewilderment running through the south Wales Police that they didn't have a steer -nor the mental wherewithal- about arresting any suspected agitator. During this skirmish, in which the neighbours were out in force relentlessly heckling the police, an immaculately uniformed Chief Commander marched over to me and my good friend, anarchic 60s biker hippie (and the first person I'd ever known who steadfastly refused to have a television in his home) Jimi.

Pointing his baton at us, and in clipped tones threatening to *"arrest the both of you for conspiracy to start a riot -unless you move on"*. Jimi retorted: *"I bet you have a good wank at night, thinking about all those police powers you've been given. You've got a hard-on now, haven't you? Fuck off, you dirty fascist perv".* The stunned superior froze and turned tail to the comfort of his ranks, with the laughter of Jimi and several residents bumping a minimalism of mockery in his ears.

I paid for it later though. Grabbed from behind as I returned from the shops and bundled into a police van for a kicking, which for me was more laughable than painful, as overweight perspiring bobbies could hardly muster any strength to deliver that corporal lesson. I stood up, and in the best tradition of Bond Villain, Jaws; calmly brushed away the dusty footprints on my t-shirt and jeans and flashed them a grin before exiting. Call it a draw, lads. The bastards kept my shopping though.

Anyway, everyone had enough on their hands trying to extinguish the conflagration that miners had set on the freshly cut dry grassy roundabout, which caused a giant tailback on the A48 and roads in and out of the steelworks. Effectively stopping the convoy in its tracks.

The story that set the locals ablaze though came in the very early hours. My parents' house was (and still is) about 200 metres from the entrance to the steelworks where the miners' cabin was situated, and my bedroom was at the front, meaning that I could view it from the window. I recall it being about 02:45 when a whooshing boom shuddered my sleep and set the dog off yapping and pissing confusedly like it was Bonfire Night all over again. A quick shuffle of the net curtains and I could see the cabin ablaze, cinders of ash and roof pitch ascending into the night sky like intoxicated larks. I raced out to find five miners standing there, flummoxed. *"We'd only gone for a walk 'cos we was bored, and saw it explode as we was coming back, like. Bastards. I knew they'd fuckin' do this."*

Neighbours took them in for the night (apart from my Mam, who lived by the principle of *never turning a gypsy away from the door* …but damned if she was offering shelter to a miner); and in the sodden illuminate of dawn, one could review the damage. It was obliterated. A shell of charred walls, smelted tables and carbonised magazines. We implored with the police to investigate this as an arson attack, but the nonplussed constabulary hummed that it was probably a faulty gas bottle that exploded from the ignition of passing vehicles. There were no correspondingly damaged vehicles, or at least vehicles at the time, having caused or even witnessed the inferno. You'd have thought they'd stop, having just come within a hairsbreadth of demise at the inferno of a roadside bomb.

To this day, locals sympathetic to the miners insist that this was the work of Government intelligence services such as MI5 (or *'MFI'* as one neighbour exhorted, conjuring up the conspiratorial image of a mid-price furniture cartel sending a message to rivals as to whom was Top Boy). Luckily, this was decades before military drones, or otherwise the fervent lava of sedition would point to Thatcher with an Atari joystick and a 12" TV, directing a pinpoint airstrike on this band of scruffy rogues as her panties became soaked in the bloodlust.

But even if it was an accident caused by domestic negligence, it did have a lasting effect: it drew a line across the pickets' presence; causing many of them to withdraw and find other ways of activism, e.g., appearing unannounced or *flying* other mass gatherings. The group of men with whom I'd formed a bond playing cricket and collecting mushrooms dissolved. My temporary friends had departed, and in my own fickle way, there was no impetus for keeping in touch. I never saw them again, and often wonder how they survived this and how they assimilated into a post-industrial landscape of enterprise zones and small factories built adjacent to the pits that were ruthlessly flooded by the callous architects of their passing.

How can we evaluate the lives of miners and their communities through the prism of strikes? Can we at all? The feet of working-class struggle and socialism are held by the bindings of history. There would be no public sector without the likes of politicians who cut their teeth as miners or industrial workers and lived in worlds where the essential foundations to life improvement were unaffordable. No NHS. No free housing. No universal education. No worker and human rights. No safety. No pensions.

Left to the *trickle-down* big Con, we'd still be eating dog meat and pulling out each other's teeth. The scars of sorrow are tattooed in the lungs, skin, and frowns of those who hacked razor shards of anthracite from the surface of seams buried deep in the bowels of the Earth, and the wives who would live in generational poverty and watch helpless as their husbands, fathers, brothers and sons wasted into gaunt shells riddled with the cancers and lung rot of Black Gold. Photos of those no longer with us mirror the sad, beaten but defiant faces of famous 19th century native Americans you see staring back from coffee table photobooks nestling adjacent to bowls of wax fruit in a showhome.

But all this history is discarded like a blood-coughed tissue and re-dressed in the framework of a strike that lasted only twelve months. In that time, they were labelled *'The Enemy Within'*, beaten and subjugated by the sheer weight of a system that set about dehumanising them. They were not *one of us.* They were a different breed to hard-working aspirational 80s people. An ugly aboriginal genus living on sodden grey hilltops that nobody ever visits out of fear. A culture that had to be eradicated by whatever means necessary to preserve a way of life that now encompassed greed and sociopathic decadence. The same language you hear now from the mouths of grifting racists dedicated to drowning cross-channel refugees.

When the Welsh miners, the most steadfast in resistance to the very last man and woman (Merthyr Tydfil was widely considered to be the strongest community in support of the strike of any mining area in Britain) decided that it was time to give up starvation, march back to work and a certain scarified future of job loss and infertility, it was a proud display that was heart-breaking to observe. Many in the UK hated the Tories for what they had done to people who had carried the power and prosperity of our post-war nation on their broken curved backs for generations, keeping the lights on while the lights went out in their own eyes. Indifference set in like knotweed as the public -egged on by the reactionary press- grew increasingly weary of the dispute. The final death knell for the movement came via a tragic act of mindless desperation on November 30th, 1984, when two striking miners dropped a 46lb concrete block from Rhymney Road bridge, killing taxi driver and father of four David Wilkie; who, accompanied by police outriders, was ferrying suspected scabs to work at the local mine.

The Strike divides us to this day, and the miserable obstinate shadow of Scargill mystifyingly posits a Marley's Ghost on any Labour politician or trade union leader daring to be radical. I still have numerous school friends who sit on either bank of the river Discourse, never agreeing with the reasons and consequences of a depressing saga. Maybe the only way to settle this argument is via a pithy thought: How many libraries did the miners build? And how many did the Tories close down?

Chapter 11: What is Left?

November is always the month that this nation indulges in a spot of collective angst, naval-gazing, and accusatory finger-pointing; trembling hands hover nervously over a collection tin, wondering if the poppy is still significant in this day and age where homeless, hypothermic ex-soldiers question where their next meal is coming from. Marks of respect and solidarity nowadays come in the form of garish rubber wristbands, and those unlucky enough to get contact dermatitis from wearing the bloody things would probably set up a Facebook page or something. The less IT-literate among us may even hang a bedsheet from the nearest bridge with a crudely daubed slogan, leaving it to dissolve in the elements, with the painted letters running like the mascara of a drunken divorcee.

The poppy has evoked a series of debates about its relevancy. After all, its primary purpose is to commemorate a war that happened over 90 years ago (with subsequent wars and conflicts bolted onto it for good measure, like an old car supplemented with extra parts scavenged over the years to keep the rust bucket roadworthy). Media commentators and public figures rightly question the pressure of wearing a small red paper flower and the apparent BBC edict to do so, likening the societal backlash to not wearing one to *'poppy fascism,"* a stupid term given the historic episodes.

The problem arises from the expectation that you *should* wear a poppy, especially if you have a respectable job, i.e., teacher, nurse, civil servant, newsreader, or lawyer (I made the last one up). To not do so would hardly result in a terse lecture about being eaten by rats while suffering the twin evils of mustard gas and trench foot, but it would probably result in a raised eyebrow and some huffing in those morning office team meetings. One year I bought three poppies, simply because it was obvious that they were going to become detached by coats, seatbelts, etc. However, my third purchase was on November 11, and having a meeting that morning, do you think I could find a bugger anywhere? The blind dread that engulfed me was totally unnecessary. If we don't want to wear a bloody poppy, then we shouldn't feel guilty about it. Equally, if we want to imitate some fatuous bloat on an ITV reality show, fork out 85 quid, and become adorned with the latest jewel-encrusted designer effort the size of a mule's head, then that should be OK too. Shouldn't it?

I've always been anti-war. The blood-soaked follies of Iraq and Afghanistan have proven that in certain given circumstances, war is a tool oft-used to promote the vested commercial and imperial interests of national bullies who would probably soil themselves at the sound of a lawnmower backfiring. War is akin to a load of drunken lads gate-crashing a house party, raiding the fridge, pissing in the aquarium, shagging the host, and beating up her boyfriend before setting fire to the pet dog, who trails a frenzy of burning shit across the lounge. They then up and depart, leaving a smouldering aftermath of chaos and emotional debris that takes aeons to repair.

However unavoidable war is, one cannot doubt the fortitude of those who have to face death. We've all had what we consider to be woeful traumatic events in our lives that we'd all prefer to avoid and forget: car accidents, fights, relationship breakdowns, financial worries, erectile dysfunction (or was that just me?). But how can this even scratch the surface of a daily fight for survival in conditions that would pollute the Gates of Hell, surrounded by the tumefied decaying cadavers of friends we once sat next to in school, learning our ABCs, chasing around the yard, catching butterflies, climbing trees, swapping cards, nicking sweets from the corner shop? How could we even begin to fathom the sense of helplessness that young men feel when they are sent out each day with the thought that they may never return alive to feel the glow of a lover next to them or enjoy the warmth of the summer sun on a quiet Sunday afternoon snoozing in the garden?

My great-grandfather stands as the reason why I wear a poppy every year. Private Sydney Hooper ('Pop') was a gentle, unassuming man who liked to sing little limericks to a four-year-old boy with shiny eyes who sat on his knee and demanded to see the bullet wound in his right hand and examine the World War I gallantry medal nestling in a small velvet-lined wooden case. These twin trophies were evidently the consequence of his capture of a pillbox armed to the teutonic teeth with a nest of machine guns, as legend would have it. More impressive was his uncharacteristic anger at the rise of fascism, and despite his experience of the trenches, was at the front of the queue to sign up for the International Brigades to fight Franco. Luckily for Pop, my horrified (and exasperated) great Nan bribed a local copper with a packet of sausages to arrest him on a trumped-up charge of loitering to stop him heading to Spain with other ideological -but fatally misguided- men and women.

Pop never spoke much about the *Great War* or the effect it had on him. A small child could never comprehend PTSD or *'shell-shock'*. I remember those days at the height of 1967, and *The Summer of Love*. He would take me up to Bethany Square, where there were lines of benches occupied by his old comrades, many of whom had eye patches, empty sleeves where arms once were, refashioned bases of walking sticks to replace legs lost on the fields of Ypres and Somme, and faces spattered with a myriad of black and red holes. To a man, they were rendered deaf from the constant artillery bombardment, as the local air filled with the high-pitched whistling of mistuned hearing aids. Yet they still retained a sense of quiet dignity and perspective. Bitterness never entered the lexicon of their discourse. Every one of them oozed with the essences of enduring politeness, optimism, and kindness. In the face of a sixties counterculture that railed against the establishment and its tools of war, these old men never argued with the idealistic hip kids that confronted them, preferring to agree with them that war was and is wrong;   and despite the huge generational and cultural differences, won them around.   The bizarre sight of iridescent long-haired youngsters joyously chewing the fat (and an endless supply of boiled sweets) with old mutilated men who'd spat in the face of Satan will stay in my mind for always.

In the intervening months and years, Bethany Square featured less and less of Pop's friends; dissolving like the embers of a rain-soaked fire. In 1969, pneumonia took him to them. Even then, he departed with quiet dignity. His last performance was crawling breathlessly along the landing to the top of the stairs in a Father Christmas outfit to sprinkle more dust of wonderment on his little great-grandson standing at the foot, tears in his dying eyes illuminated by the beam from my face. Bertrand Russell once wrote: *War does not determine who is right - only who is left.*   I love and miss him every day, and can only wonder what he would think about my hatred of the sneering violent callous something-for-nothing superficial venal country we live in today. He would probably take me to one side and lighten the mood with another limerick. Lest we forget.

And best we forget that if anyone these days could actually be bothered to thumb through historical text, immersing themselves in fusty chronicles (probably handled by an officious-looking man clad in snooker ref's gloves) one would be able to recount tales of triumph and misadventure bobbing in a sea of adversity. We would witness how historical failures would be fabled in an almost shrug-shouldered acceptance that it was ever thus. When King Harold was about to be rendered into bite-sized kebabs on the fields of Hastings, he pursed his lips and offered his arrow-sieved head for Norman butchers. When a mud and disease-caked tommy clambered out of some dysenteric Flanders foxhole to be gassed and bayoneted in the face by advancing Germans, his last words were probably a cheeky *"Cor blimey, Kaiser lad, yer've got me dead to rights -and make no bloomin' mistake."*

Of course, this is all bollocks. But the reason I mention it is to illuminate a contrast between the daring heroic sagas that filled the two-colour pages of latter-day childhood adventure comics, such as Victor and Eagle, in comparison to the blubbering effete milquetoast wastrels that haunt our society today.

We now live in the lachrymose generation; a place in time where the tear duct has dominion. These days it's as ubiquitous as silver nox bullets in a local park to witness grown adults suddenly erupt forth with a whining outburst as soon as the TV cameras are pointed in the direction of their pointless self-indulgent stupid moist little faces. This odious display is designed purely to pull the public along on their pissy-pants daytime cart of histrionics, seemingly expectant of a huge societal "*Aw, blesssssss*" as we huddle together doggy-paddling in a huge saline lake of sentiment. Where indomitable spirit and a cheerful disposition kept us collective under the twin sieges of disease and war, now a sense of togetherness is fostered by the daily domestic anguish of a nondescript reality TV reject who claws at our senses, wiping away grizzled snot while publicly exposing their hideous psychological entrails. Whatever happened to esperance?

These hell riders of the emotional rollercoaster attack in various guises, and include:

a) The semi-literate talent show auditionee whose IQ and ability to hold a tune is in direct ratio to the amount of fake gold sovereigns and home-brew tattoos on display. Upon the inevitable rejection, they spontaneously inflate into something resembling the critical mass of a wailing marmoset's bladder, before erupting forth in a tsunami of repugnant self-pity, proclaiming: *"this is my life... it's all I've ever dreamed of"*, while clutching a small picture of an ill child. Oh yeah. What sort of life ambition can be measured by public ridicule from a sleazy millionaire in chest-hugging trousers and some slightly movable celebrity mannequins?

b) The sporting icon who, following an embarrassing and ill-conceived comeback, hastily calls a press conference to announce -to anyone still interested- that they will be retiring again. This is then punctuated by some clichéd platitude such as *"I gave it my best shot, but it didn't work out..."* before the statement trails off as the sniffling deadbeat croaks a barely audible *"sorry"*, puts his/her hand over the microphone and dabs at a big invisible tear. And, just in case there's anyone still interested who hasn't torn out their own spleen, the washout reappears in 6 months to hold another press conference to announce to a shocked world that they regularly took drugs ...and the whole rotten melodrama is repeated ad nauseam until they suffer a fatal coronary on a minor satellite TV channel while attempting a minority sport tenuously associated with their former selves.

c) The former whatever-list celebrity venturing to glean soulful catharsis by spilling their guts on a prime-time chat show. This usually consists of a revelatory checklist featuring abuse, addiction, terminal illness or the death of a family member. The motherlode of tabloid gold is mined if all of the above apply. Most of us meander about our lives in ennui, marginally concerned about a bald tyre or if that third piece of toast was really necessary, our memory banks barely recalling that time we saw a cat licking itself on next door's sun lounger. Celebrities, however, drag themselves torn through mascara-stained battlefields of brutal gang rape, crystal meth rehab, recovery from Stage 4 cancer and *"I never got the chance to say goodbye to my mam..."*. Maybe if they'd spent less days mewling to assorted TV hosts and cheap glossy shelf tat they might just have been able to pop into see their mother in her twilight hours. Presumably for a quick selfie from the open bodybag. Fuck off.

Of course, it hasn't always been like this. Our culture never yearned for a rasorial pick at the tender scabs and weep at every available opportunity like some hired mourner at the funeral of angst. We can trace the genesis of this disease of the poignant gland to two significant events: the 1990 World Cup Semi Final, and the 1997 death of Princess Diana.

Under normal circumstances, we'd shun the moron Gascoigne, despite his staggering footballing talent. However, a mistimed tackle in Turin moved him out of the pantheon of great-but-flawed footballers and onto the laps of cooing maternalism. It's a widely held view that Gazza was crying for England when he received the booking that would potentially cost his team dearly. Bollocks. His shirt wrung out tears of self-pity because the uber dullard wasn't going to be playing in the World Cup Final. He was crying for himself. However, as an almost weird echo of wartime propaganda, created to boost the nation's morale (such as the collection of metal items from households to *help the war effort*, even though it was all dumped in a large incinerator or ended up as Grace Jones), the press played on it as *Gazza's Tears for Unlucky England*. At the stroke of a journo's pen, he went from drunken Geordie amoeba to some sort of patriotic deity who, as a man (albeit one wearing fake tits), was not afraid to shed real tears for Albion.

Gazza has a lot to answer for, because since that time we've had to endure the public nausea (and continual book sales) of a whimpering cohort of cloggers, banging on at length about their own self-built obstacles with lager, bookmakers and marching powder. And where exactly are we supposed to feel pity for a millionaire Arsenal footballer so hammered that he passed out behind the wheel of a car and ploughed into a lamppost? Unfortunately, Ann Widdecombe wasn't frozen in the oncoming headlights; otherwise, he would've been knighted for services.

Diana's death was an illustration of societal illness and moral panic. Almost as if we'd kept a grizzling genie that looked like Stan Laurel handcuffed under the stiffness of our upper lips. When this pampered Sloane (who was not averse to performing the doe-eyed Bambi routine herself) died in the Pont de l'Alma tunnel in Paris, a surge of fervid lava engulfed us like the unfortunates of Pompeii, but with plastic union flags. Drowning under a sea of Interflora and Elton John, we all enlisted to grab an even bigger slice of the sentimental pie than the next person. Thus, we witnessed crazed scenes of scuffles breaking out in Woolworths as grown humans battled to grab as many copies of '*Candle in the Wind* as possible like fruit pickers at a doomsday harvest. Groups of complete strangers shared bodily fluids as shoulders were used to wipe away the mucosal discharge of a million dolorous group hugs.

The most abhorrent facet of Di's death was the overwhelming compulsion to grieve for her. Overnight, the country turned into the closing scene from a Romero movie as red-eyed zombies shuffled aimlessly about our towns and cities, moaning and dribbling, and attacking those who remained ambivalent to this plague of contrition. My son was six when Diana died, and his school insisted that all the children painted posters of remembrance, which would then be sent to Buckingham Palace. Whereas concocted beatific scenes of an ickle Princess, with wings ascending to the heavens were *de rigeur* for the Palace bonfire; my lad opted for the Francis Bacon approach and produced a black diptych featuring a melting coffin emblazoned with "*Rest In Pieces*". I was later called for discussion with a *concerned* headmaster.

But where do we go from here? Is the Maldives at risk of being submerged due to global warming or the voluminous crocodile tears from a national outpouring of faux dejection? Can precipitation be blamed upon failing celebs on an Instagram self-help weekend in Snowdonia? Are the Tracks of My Tears about to be taken over by Network Rail? Please don't ask me anymore ...I feel as though I'm starting to well up ...er... (croak) sorry, I...er (sniff)....

Chapter 12: Down the Tubes

What neural egg chamber birthed our cynicism and hardened crispy shells? Media stories about chlorinated chicken imported from the US brought back a whiff of memories from dinners in state primary school. In this case, the life-changing cuisine villain was liver and mash. This brown mulch of organ centrifuge came in square shapes replete with protruding arteries, like some hideous gravy-covered roadkill from a Quatermass movie. The dinner ladies, no doubt knowing a thing or two about presentation, whacked it onto our plates like a karate auctioneer.

The real gastronomy treat though, was reserved for the *scraping bowl,* a large metal receptacle into which we would dispose of our uneaten food in the knowledge that local pig farms could share in the misery. The sight of a 3-foot-high, tottering tower of liver on the cusp of wintle haunts my taste buds to this day, to the extent that any attempt to serve me offal-based cuisine would have to come as part of a package including a tranquiliser dart and three months of post-traumatic counselling.

But what was it about school dinners that provoked a sense of communal revulsion? Was it the sight of Mr Lewis, the deputy headmaster reaching first for the custard jug -only for an erroneous nasal hair dropping into the yellow void? Was it the realisation that, at some stage, a pea with the outer strata of an asteroid would hit the bossy girl tucking into her flame-seared gypsy tart (it took me four attempts)? Was it the angry dinner ladies serving a lifetime rehabilitative programme decreed by the Nuremburg trials?

Who cares? School dinners were a rite of passage, alongside putting a turd in the caretaker's mop bucket and stapling the posh kids' duffel coats to the desk.

It's what made us what we are as adults in this country today: bitter, downhearted empty souls gazing out through a cracked window of despair as the clouds of hopelessness drift by, raining tears of lost ambition. Turkey twizzlers, anyone?

Epilogue

"We inherit from our ancestors gifts so often taken for granted... Each of us contains within... this inheritance of soul. We are links between the ages, containing past and present expectations, sacred memories and future promise." –Edward Sellner.

Thoughts tailspin to halcyon days where things mattered, personalities feted, individuality for the purpose of goodwill cherished and decency was a feast for all. These aphorisms became separated from their families, herded into remote warehouses, strung up and butchered; and the rendered carcasses driven off late at night in a bus marked *'Lost'*. In generations to come social historians with no eyelids will uncover mass quicklime graves, being able only to identify the wretched bodies of the hopeless through rotting dental records barely held together with the putrified tartare of Monster Munch. Carbon dating will construct a picture of when *there was such a thing as society.* And they will laugh so hard, like the tinfoil aliens from the Smash commercials at how fucking stupid we were throwing it all away.

Cynicism now leaks like effluent from the pores of our streets. Take a look outside. Lateral blurs from warped elliptical bodies stuffed in polyester slowly cross your sightlines. Puffing and sweating rotisserie blimps waddle towards thrift circuses and pastry galleries; years of elephantine self-neglect and abuse-by-proxy etched in scowls barely masked by ascending blueberry plumes of exhaled vape. Faces reddened with injurious anticipation of another day spent hoping for something and blaming someone else if they don't get it, with exertion and sacrifice long discarded in a graveyard of verbs and textile static; their yellowing decay strangled by the grubbing weeds of corruption, lies and fraud. Trickle down. Trickle down.

You're stuck in a gridlock of your mind. A temperate day of incalescence ebbing and flowing amidst that rain which penetrates the marrow of a finger attempting to paint crude spurting cocks on a misted window. The outside road is wheezing tarmac steam like the uncontrolled puff from an old rigger's armpits. Stuck here. No movement. Rainbow asphalt puddles flicker marine tones like the etching chlorides of despondency. Sometimes there comes a virus blown on the backs of doomed husks that bestows dominion on a select few clawing their way through narrow apertures of naked ambition, pulping a wake of withered effigies that once burned with the lights of imagination, colour and song.

We can use the onrushing death train to embrace the inevitable denouement to our careers and lives, before retreating into a hermetic Sudoku cryogenesis; our grubby emaciated frames silhouetted in the halogen from a Currys doorway, staring into a dark star through giant abandoned apertures where eyes once were.

The concept writhes like a kitten on razor wire. A nation in binding, ready for rehab and therapy after a terminal *thumbs down* by baronets lubricated at Bullingdon, toasting crumpets on the arse cheeks of the ignorant; peeking from their turrets to spit semi-congealed ptarmigan onto the salivating masses below. Never was so much given by so many to so few absolute wankers.

But while cities burn and minimum wage passport officers are pounded under the feet of angry sun worshippers desperate to escape their sodden stalags, we give a collective shrug, and tut as if we'd just seen a single mother light a Cuban cigar in Home Bargains. They say that when someone's about to die, their life and past furniture flashes before them. Well, maybe the reality is just a purgatory of boredom by proxy waiting for a signal that never comes. And the light goes out.

And on that chirpy note: look out for Book 2 for further tat amidst the wreckage. Including adrenaline-fuelled thrills with the NHS, football, gigs, school, alcohol, self-image, and discovering (unsurprisingly) how navigating sex can be as perilous as any foothill eroded by those who came before.

It's been a pleasure. Feel free to disagree.

About The Author

Antony S.Thomas has been a mostly workshy writer and cartoonist for numerous magazines and fanzines down the aeons. He has written many film and music reviews, and boxing reportage.

When he's not attempting to string random sentences together, he can be discovered at his Monmouthshire home messing around with ambient sounds under the guise of Observation Point, haunting BBC Radio stations with dark shadows of creeping melancholy.

He once ran a now-defunct podcast show of eclectic music, Paradox Room (all episodes are available for streaming on Mixcloud). Nobody listened.

"Massive chin ...bananaface." Clinton Baptiste, paranormal explorer.

"Some twat from West Glamorgan calling him/herself 'A S Thomas'." John Peel.

"Mike Tyson can knock you out ...anytime." An old drunk in Swansea bus station.

"Fancy a pint?" Timothy Dalton (I declined. Couldn't be arsed)

"That cute Welsh guy." Brix Smith.

"Fuck off!" Jools Holland, Swansea Top Rank 1978.

If you enjoyed this book (or hated it and want to fight), please contact the author via:

Web: observationpoint.co.uk
Email: asthomas1963@yahoo.com
Instagram/Threads: Antony Thomas